The Bride &
The Blood Covenant
Ceremony

By Jamie Carte

*Keep Getting Ready,
Jesus Is Coming!
Jamie Carte*

xulon
PRESS

The Bride & The Blood Covenant Ceremony
by Jamie Carte

Printed in the United States of America

ISBN 9781626974036

www.xulonpress.com

I dedicate this Book to my beautiful Mother,
Carol Elizabeth Webb.

Mom left Earth and moved to Heaven while I was writing this Book on 12 November 2012. Mom you have impacted me in so many ways. I am forever looking for you and hearing your voice in my life. I await when I shall see you again. You are not in my past, you are in my future. I love you so much and I am proud to call you my Mom. And as we both would always say before we hung up on the phone, "I'll see you later!"

CONTENTS

FOREWORD

*H*ello World! It is my honor and privilege to be the first
to introduce to you, the Love of My Life, Jamie Renee
Carte. As Jamie's husband I get to experience the full anointing
that God has on her life. And anointed she is! Jamie has used
her life experiences to help craft this book and write it in a way
that expresses her unwavering love for God and His Covenant
with us, His People. Jamie draws upon life experiences that
were very hard on her and has turned that around to give her
life to The Lord Jesus and serve Him openly and boldly for the
last twenty one years of her beautiful life.

Jamie has overcome many obstacles in her life. God has
delivered Jamie from many things, including alcoholism and
drug abuse. One of the most difficult obstacles was an attack
Satan had against her in the form of an "incurable" disease.
When God brought Jamie and I together, the Doctors had
already told Jamie that she was dying. Some said I had everything to lose with being with Jamie, but I knew that she was
my mate from God and that God would heal her. And praise
be To Jesus, Jamie is healed and whole and my life has been
totally blessed ever since!

God has used Jamie in many different ministries in her
life such as Youth Minister, Praise and Worship Leader,
Singer, Bible Teacher, Prophet, Preacher, Evangelist and
now a Writer! Anything that God calls Jamie to do, she puts
her whole heart and attention to that task and I think you will
notice this as you read this Book. One thing that I love about

Jamie is her passion for God, His Kingdom, and His Truths. Great revelation is within this Book. Passion is in this Book. Vast details of God and mankind's history are in this Book.

Do you remember when you were younger being in a classroom, a Sunday School class or a family member reading to you? While they read to you, do you remember picturing what the words described to you in the story were? Or maybe you have memories of you, yourself reading a book and the images you would form in your mind would stay with you? It was like you would form the literal picture of what the book being read looked like. Well, that is what you are about to experience all over again as you read this Book that you hold.

This Book is truly a specific and detailed account of the history of God's Love and His Passion for His People. Upon the many hours of research done to deliver to you this Book, Jamie found the extraordinary actions of God and man in their Love for one another. When you read this Book you will embark on a journey that will take you in time from the beginning to the end of God's passion for people and you will see the passion man has displayed throughout history responding back to God

I must say that at times this Book will shock you in what you will discover. And as I said earlier the imagery you will see in your mind as you read the words will at times astonish you. Yet, what you will come away with by the message and love that's within these pages is just that, you will see clearly what lengths God will go to and has, just to be with you.

I pray that you enjoy this work from The Lord as Jamie, by The Holy Spirit will take you back in history and give you a vivid view of Love, pure Love in this very deep subject. Though at first what you will begin to learn may sound strange to you, I urge you to keep reading, for the revelations that you will experience will come, one by one. Until you totally see from the past all the way to the present of how rich Blood Covenant is and has always been. If you really want to see the expense that you and I were to purchase, you must see the process and cost that the Buyer (The Lord) went through to get what or WHO (The Bride) He was purchasing.

It has been my privilege to introduce to you my love, Jamie. I seen Jamie birth this first Book on The King's behalf and on your behalf. One thing that I love about Jamie is her passion for God, His Kingdom and His Truths. As a Prophet, God has gifted her to be able to "go behind the curtain" of things and bring out beautiful Truths for His Bride. This Book was written to help The Bride understand God's Love for us and the relationship He wants to have with us.

Thank you for reading this and we pray this Book blesses and enlightens you to God's complex but simple Love for you His Bride! This has been a totally biased Foreward for the woman of my dreams Jamie Renee Carte from her husband Dewayne Hurston Carte! *I love you Jamie! And I'm so very proud of you!* Thanks for joining us on this journey and God Bless you in all your ways!

Dewayne H. Carte
President of Jamie Carte Ministries (JCM)

ACKNOWLEDGMENTS

I want to acknowledge and give Glory and Credit to Whom this Book would not have true meaning if it were not for Him, my Best Friend and Big Brother, Jesus The Christ from Nazareth. Sir, it is Your Blood and Your Life and sacrifice that not only made this Book possible, but life and life more abundantly for billions of people! Lord, You are my Hero and The One Who rescued me out of darkness and despair. I love You, Jesus! You are truly The One and Only Covenant Representative and The Best of Heaven! Thank You Master, for being with me and encouraging me to write this Book.

To my beautiful husband, Dewayne Carte, I cannot thank you enough for all that you are to me and all that you do for me. I am a better person, woman and Minister because of you! God has blessed me in my life and I know that because of you. You are a man of men and I adore you. Your strength, courage and consistency have not only taught me how to live life, it has also brought joy that I did not know until you. You truly are my knight in shining armor! Thank you for loving me like Christ loves His Church. I love you Baby!

To my precious family Jimmy Webb, Tonya Webb and Kristy Webb who have encouraged me and prayed for me and graciously gave me the separated time that it took to write this Book. I know that Mom leaving Earth has changed our lives forever. And I want you each to know that I am always there for you and I support your dreams and always will. I am a blessed woman to have such a great father and two amazing sisters that I have! I look forward to our future together! Thank you for loving me like you do! I love you so very much!

To Jerry and Debbie Legg and Bill and Donna Legg, I must say, I love you all very much! You are so special to Dewayne and me. We could not have finished this book without your support and prayers. You were with us through it all. When the enemy attacked in the midst of writing this Book, you were there. When we needed to just release and cry out loud, you were there. When I finished writing the Book, you were there and celebrated us doing so! What fantastic examples of The Lord's disciples you are. You are our family and we love you!

To Jennifer West, Brenda Ferrell, Pam Bigham, Pricilla Wills and Corrie Forsythe we thank you with all of our hearts for all of the prayers and intercession you have done on our behalf for the writing and completion of this Book. Your covering and undergirding is what propelled us and all that it took to accomplish this mission for The Master. Together, we did it guys! Your role and passion played such a crucial part in this assignment. We love you and appreciate you our precious Prayer Warriors for The Kingdom!

To the Jamie Carte Ministries Board of Directors, Launa Swain, Tonya Lowe and Tonya Webb, you have all three prayed for me and encouraged me for not just a day, not for just months, but for years to complete this first Book. You have heard me talk about it and cry about it and you've seen me even at times resist the notion that I could even do this! I know that besides Dewayne, you have seen the struggle I had with completing this project. And through it all you have loved me and told me that I could do this. You have been there. . . always been there. You are consistently there for me and for Dewayne and for the needs of JCM. We, together with you are more than just a Board over a Ministry, we are family. I don't know how to thank you for all that you do. . . what a fantastic group of ladies you are in my life. I thank God for you my sisters and friends!

To the Jamie Carte Ministries Covenant Partners and Friends, you are the rock that Dewayne and I and JCM stand on. Thank you for your faithfulness to God and His Mission and Call on this Ministry and thank you for ALL OF THE PRAYERS AND SUPPORT that you have given us! We are with you and for you and are forever fighting the good fight of faith with you! We are in Covenant with you and will ALWAYS be here for you, covering you with The Word of God and Professions of faith every day.

I want to especially thank Rebecca Brogan from John The Baptist Artworks (JTBA) who blessed us with her beautiful pictures for this Book. Rebecca, you are such a talent for The King! Thank you for sharing your wonderful gift from God in your drawings. You so unselfishly gave JCM freedom to use your pictures so that others could see meanings behind the words written in this Book. I pray that The Lord bless you and your Ministry indeed! We could not thank you enough!

Thank you, Pastor Mitchell Bias and the Congregation of Regional Church of God of Delbarton, WV. Pastor Bias, you are such an example to Dewayne and I and a Father in The Lord to us who we have always been able to run home to. When Mom left Earth, you RCOG, were there for us and displayed God to us in so many ways. Pastor Bias and RCOG's encouragement and unconditional love is amazing! We stand taller because of you Pastor and the incredible Body of Believers of Regional! Thank you RCOG for always being there for us! We love you RCOG Body!

Thank you, Debbie Legg for all that you do to serve at Jamie Carte Ministries. You are a picture of a servant of Jesus Christ. I could not have written this Book without you! You are a diligent and passionate follower of Jesus Christ and your attention to His Ministry is marvelous! You kept everything at JCM running smoothly during the writing of this Book and do so at all times. No job task is too big, too hard or too dirty for you. . . you will serve Jesus no matter what! What a true joy you are to me in my life! I love you Debbie!

To Kenneth and Gloria Copeland, thank you for your faithfulness and being spiritual parents to Dewayne and me. It was through you and your Ministry that I first heard of The Blood

Covenant Ceremony and after praying about it, your Ministry sent me a teaching just out of the blue one day on The Blood Covenant, though I never wrote or called you for it! God knew that I had to know and begin a journey of studying on this and used you to get me started. Though Dewayne and I have not had the privilege to meet you in person yet, we have sat under you and loved you for many years from afar. We love you and are in Covenant with you!

WHEN EVERYTHING
CHANGED FOR ME

*O*ne very special day something happened to me that up until this point in my life, I really cannot recall ever happening any time before. I had what some would call an open vision. It was as if I was not in my present place or in the present time. It was as if I had been transported from where I was to another place. I will describe it to the best of my ability so that you can picture what I saw.

I was walking very slowly into a room. It was a room that I had never seen or been in before. The room was very dark, so dark that I would hold my hands out to the side of me as I walked, feeling my way through the darkness of this room. I could see shadows moving across the walls of the dark room as I continued to walk. There was what I would describe as a foggy or smoky presence in the room. The combination of the darkness, the shadows and the foggy or smoky matter made my movement within this room very slow and cautious.

I kept thinking to myself, *Where am I?* Yet I do not recall having any fear. It was if I was on a search for something as I moved very slowly within the darkness of that room. I came around a corner and could see something ahead of me. Ahead of me in the darkness I saw a wall that was made of rock or stone. Many stones were in this wall. The wall looked very old, crumbled and very, very thick. As I moved toward the wall I noticed a large hole carved out at the bottom center. As

I moved toward the rock wall and the large hole in it, I could see something was sticking out of the dark hole.

I slowly moved toward the hole in the wall in that darkness. As I walked I would look to my right and left and see the movement of the shadows on the wall. Though it was very dark, you could still see those shadows moving. As I approached the hole in the rock wall, I began to identify what was laying outside of the hole. . . IT WAS A SET OF A WOMAN'S LEGS! The woman was on the ground inside that hole and her legs were bent slightly to the side from the knees. She was barefoot. Her legs and her feet were very dirty and stained. There was dried blood that had run down her legs prior to me seeing her. Those legs were battered, bruised and covered with dark dirt. Draped over her knees was a torn and tattered dress. The dress that she had on had a shredded look to it and was very dirty. It appeared that the original color was white, but it was so darkened with dirt, it now showed multiple grays and black in places. I could only see the legs of the woman sticking out of the hole. I could not see her body or face. The rest of her body and being was within the hole and hidden in its darkness.

As I moved closer to that hole, I had the thought come to me, *Oh, she's in trouble; I must help her!* I remember feeling great compassion for this woman, for I knew that she had been abused somehow and she needed help. I finally made my way through the darkness and to the hole in the rock wall. I knew that I had to help her. I bent over and reached my hand toward the woman in the hole to help her, and when I reached out, she quickly pulled her dirty legs and feet within the hole with the rest of her body. I knew within myself she was afraid of anyone helping her, so she hid herself quickly in the hole.

I was then taken from that dark place to another room. I found myself standing behind a magnificent large chair. The chair had golden sides and a high back that had red velvet material on it. The chair looked like a throne that a king would sit upon. My own hair was no longer flowing to my shoulders; it was now twirled and fixed upon my head. My hair had salt and pepper color on it now and I had on what seemed to be a woman's business suit with a skirt. I knew that I was dressed up for something special.

To the right of the kingly chair was a beautiful mirror. The mirror also had gold all around it. It was the only thing I could really see to the right of me. The mirror was very close to the kingly, high-backed chair. As I looked into the mirror, I saw great light illuminating and reflecting in the mirror. The light from the beautiful mirror was brilliant and simply dazzling! The light seemed to not only be IN the mirror but surging and flowing OUT of the mirror! It was as if I could feel the light coming from the mirror!

Then suddenly I turned to look in front of me and now sitting in the stunning chair was a beautiful bride! She sat very comfortably in the kingly, tall chair. The bride was very relaxed and I knew, as did she, that she was sure of herself and her position while sitting in the chair. She was so peaceful. I stood behind her and the chair. I knew that I had been with this bride many times before. She was familiar with me and I was very at ease and familiar with her. She had on a bridal gown that was white and her hair was styled beautifully upon her head. There was a white glow coming from her gown. As I stood behind her as she sat in that chair, I had such a love for her and felt as though she was very close to me, like family. I knew within me as I stood there behind her that I had spent much time with her, instructing and teaching this bride. I felt that I had poured myself into her and she was a part of me sitting there.

I then placed both of my hands on her shoulders from behind her, and I recall touching that white wedding gown on those shoulders of hers. While having both hands on her shoulders, I then bent towards her ears and said softly to her, "It's time, Sweetie!" When I said those words, the bride immediately arose to her feet. When she stood, great beams of light came from all over her being! I stood amazed at what I was witnessing! I quickly looked to my right again and saw nothing but an abundance of light coming from the mirror, pure astounding light, and that light was coming from the bride! The light in that mirror had been coming from her the whole time! I looked forward again and watched as she walked forward, fully shining with light, till I could see her no more, for the light was all that I could see. I knew that what I was witnessing was the bride in the Rapture. I stood there watching in total love and utter amazement and pure joy! As I stood in that beautiful room, I then heard a voice that spoke from within me say, "I want you to get My Bride from *that room* to *this room!*" As this was being said to me, I could see the first room of darkness and shadows and then I would be back in the room with the light, the mirror and where the bride was. "My Bride has been worn, abused and battered from the World and from others in The Church. And She has been cut and is dirty and tattered. I want you to get Her from that room to this room!" I can still see and hear it all as clearly as I write to you right now! I'm overwhelmed!

As soon as I came to myself, in tears, I realized what had happened and that The Lord had given me a specific assignment. Since that day, this assignment has been threaded into every fiber of my being. It's who I am. I am on a mission from The Commander-in-Chief to assist His Bride to make Herself ready for Her Wedding Day, which is The Rapture of The Church. I am Her Lady in Waiting and will continue to minister to Her as She is moving from that dark room of fear and shadows into Her faith-filled position on Her seat of royalty as The Bride of Jesus Christ that She already is. The Bride must learn who She is and live in that position She holds.

You see, Jesus came to Planet Earth once and He is truly Coming Back. I know that we have all heard this many, many times, especially if you have been in Church for any amount of time. Jesus Christ of Nazareth IS COMING very soon and He's COMING **FOR SOMEONE!** That SOMEONE is His Church, His Beautiful Bride. This is so personal, and yet so public with Him. He is longing for Her and we The Church down deep also long for Him. It's just that we are so preoccupied and divided with the World and all it has to offer us. Still, *His* devotion and attention are not divided. He thinks of us, dances over us, rejoices over us, sings over us and is preparing a place for us to come and live with Him. He's very serious about His promises and Covenant with His Bride. He has kept and is keeping His promises. He *is* building a wonderful mansion for us to live in. He *is* ever making intercession for us. He *is* coming back on a cloud with a trumpet call to raise the dead first and then those of us who are still alive will be *caught up* with Him in the air (1 Thessalonians 4:13-18).

So why write about a subject called The Blood Covenant Ceremony in lieu of ministering to The Bride of Christ? To even tap into the Wonderfulness of Him and The Love He has for His Bride, we must begin to learn *How It All Began!* We need to know how She, The Bride, Began and The Promise, The Covenant, that started it all. Go with me, friend, back into history to see how this beautiful love story began and just *how expensive The People of God really are!* We must look back so we can move forward, Church! *EVERYTHING that we are in Him began right here. . . in The Blood Covenant!*

BLOOD COVENANT

Representative is Chosen

Covenant Site is Chosen

Conditions of Covenant are Decided

On and Declared

Animal(s) is Cut

Walk of Blood

Cutting of Representative's Flesh

**Promises Proclaimed and Names
are Combined**

Giving of Coats

Trading of Belts

Covenant Meal

Please Use This Outline
Throughout The Book

Chapter One

WILL YOU MARRY ME?

f we are truly going to look back in time so that we can see who we are now as The Bride of Jesus and in the future as The Bride of Jesus, we must begin with the beautiful marriage of our Father and our Mother. Father God, Jesus The Son and The Holy Spirit are Three Persons and yet they are One. This is what is described as the Trinity. Father God has made it very clear throughout The Word that He is The Husband of Israel. Just some of the scriptures that show us that Father God is Israel's Husband are:

> Leviticus 20:6 (AMP) – *"The person who turns to those who have familiar spirits and to wizards, [being unfaithful to **Israel**'s Maker Who is her **Husband**, and thus] playing the harlot after them. . ."*

> Isaiah 54:5 (AMP) – *"For your Maker is your **Husband**— the Lord of hosts is His name—and the Holy One of Israel is your Redeemer; the God of the whole earth He is called."*

> Jeremiah 3:14 (AMP) – *"Return, O faithless children [of the whole twelve tribes], says the Lord, for I am Lord and Master and **Husband** to you, and I will take you*

[not as a nation, but individually]—one from a city and two from a tribal family—and I will bring you to Zion."

Jeremiah 23:10 (AMP) – *"For the land is full of adulterers (forsakers of God, Israel's true Husband). . ."*

Ezekiel 23:35 (AMP) – *"Therefore thus says the Lord God: Because you have forgotten Me [your divine Husband] and cast Me behind your back, therefore bear also [the consequences of] your lewdness and your harlotry."*

The scriptures above display that Father God and Israel are in Covenant or married to each other. And we know that God is our Father when we surrender our life to Him. And if He is our Father, then His Wife is our Mother! So, just like The Word reveals that Father God is married and is The Husband of Israel, The Word distinguishes Israel's identity as Mother.

Isaiah 50:1 (AMP) – *"THUS SAYS the Lord: Where is the bill of your mother's divorce with which I put her away, O Israel? Or which of My creditors is it to whom I have sold you? Behold, for your iniquities you were sold, and for your transgressions was your mother put away."*

Galatians 4:25-26 (NLT) – *"And now Jerusalem is just like Mount Sinai in Arabia, because she and her children live in slavery to the law. 26 But the other woman, Sarah, represents the heavenly Jerusalem. She is the free woman, and she is our mother." (There are several other scriptures throughout The Word that express Father God as Husband and Israel as His Wife and Bride. These are just a few.)*

Father God is our Father and Husband to Israel, our Mother. And Jesus is their Firstborn! He was birthed from Father God and Mother Israel! The Holy Spirit of Father God impregnated a young virgin who was in the bloodline of King David, the King of *Israel*; the virgin lived in *Israel* ("The Mother") and was an Israelite! Father God, through The Holy Spirit and a daughter of *Israel* ("The Mother"), Mary, birthed The First Born Son, Jesus into the Earth! And just like Father God has a Bride, so does His Son and Firstborn, Jesus! And in both, there was a Marriage or Covenant Ceremony to join Father God and His Bride and Jesus and His Bride.

A Covenant and Marriage began between Father God and Israel when Father God made a Covenant with Abraham many years ago. This Covenant began there and carried on through Isaac, Jacob, Moses, Joshua, Samuel, David, Solomon and many more - right up to Joseph, Mary, John The Baptist, Jesus, Paul and on and on until we get to you and me. Let's look at this profound Ceremony that began with Abraham that so profoundly connects us today.

Chapter Two

I Promise

Genesis 15:1 (AMP) – "After these things, the word of the Lord came to Abram in a vision, saying, Fear not, Abram, I am your Shield (Your King), your abundant compensation, and your reward shall be exceedingly great."

A Covenant between people in ancient civilizations was much more solemn than we have been taught about in today's society. The most momentous Covenant that we know of today is the marriage between a man and a woman. Though for many, the Covenant in marriage is not seen as serious or as important as it truly is. There are many who will just quit and walk away from their Covenant with one another over just about anything. The next closest thing we have to Covenant in our society is a piece of paper called a contract. These contracts are just ink, paper and a promise that many times are just ripped up.

The marvelous and yet so serious Procedure that God and man underwent throughout history in joining themselves in Covenant is set apart. We, in our society today, have a great void of knowing what occurred between God and man and many others throughout The Word of God. The Blood Covenant Ceremony is THE MOST IMPORTANT EVENT THAT CAN HAPPEN IN A PERSON'S LIFE. That Ceremony

WILL CHANGE YOUR LIFE FOREVER! The beautiful sections of The Blood Covenant Ceremony are as follows:

Blood Covenant

Representative is Chosen
Covenant Site is Chosen
Conditions of Covenant are Decided
On and Declared
Animal(s) is Cut
Walk of Blood
Cutting of Representative's Flesh
Promises Proclaimed and Names are Combined
Giving of Coats
Trading of Belts
Covenant Meal

Blood Covenant Preparations

In ancient civilizations, Covenant required the individuals or families involved to be absolute and unwavering with each other. Total loyalty is essential on the parts of both parties. The only way to get out of this Covenant was through death. Covenant in the Hebrew is the word *beriyth (ber-eeth')* OT:1285; **a compact made by passing between pieces of flesh: covenant, league. To cut, To divide.** Does that meaning surprise you? When I began my research into "Covenant" I thought, *What does* **a compact made by passing between pieces of flesh: covenant, league. To cut, To divide** *(beriyth (ber-eeth') OT:1285;) have to do with the word "Covenant" that I know?* And the further I dug in The Bible and its history of "Covenant", the more I realized that is exactly what a Covenant means! Let me show you.

Sincerely two families would decide that they would come into Covenant with each other. The strengths and weaknesses of the two families would be recognized. For example, if one family was not strong in prosperity but was strong in fighting skills, they could unite with a family that was wealthier than them and yet they could teach the other family how to fight and make better weapons. At the same time, the family with more wealth could offer the other family their wisdom on obtaining and multiplying their resources. The two families would share all they had with each other, for they were in Covenant with each other.

The Covenant that would be made was so serious that the only way to get out of it was through **death** and both families would know this going into Covenant. No one took their commitment lightly – they couldn't! In Covenant, even if one family member in a future generation did not keep their obligation concerning the Covenant, it would not nullify or change the agreement between the two Covenant families.

A representative would be selected out of each family to stand for and on behalf of their family. And a representative would be selected from the other Covenant family to stand for their family, just as in the first family. If the one Covenant family was strong in money and possessions, then that family would send as their representative "the banker" or the one who was the best at making, keeping or multiplying their wealth. If the other Covenant family was strong in fighting, they would bring forth their representative who was the greatest and most strategic "warrior." Whatever the families had strength in, the representatives chosen would exemplify that strength.

Both representatives chosen by each family would be the best examples of what each one of these two families could bring to the other family. These two representatives would be able and have the authority to negotiate and collaborate with each other on behalf of their own family. It was a high honor, yet a humbling position to be in as one of these representatives.

At the "negotiations," the representatives and the elders of the two families meet and discuss and decide on the Conditions of the Covenant. This meeting is where the discussions are held between the two families. It is very important. The families decide at this meeting to go where the other family goes. The families choose to go and fight when the other family goes out to battle. The families come to a decision that if the other is hungry or thirsty they promise to feed, clothe, and provide for the other under any circumstance. It is settled that what one family has is shared with the other family. Both families recognize that they have each other and will never have to stand alone again.

Also at this meeting, the Condition of getting a *new name* is agreed upon. If one family's name is Smith and the other family's name is Jones, then the two families will no longer be called by those names. They would merge their names and be called, for example, the Smithjones family or the Jonesmith family. Both families would receive this *new name* and they would surrender their former names of Smith and Jones.

The next detail to be decided upon by the two families is a site or location in which the Covenant will formally take place. The destination that is chosen will be a location that will allow all members of each family to come and witness the Covenant Ceremony. This is the Covenant Site. The number of all members of the families on both sides could be in the hundreds or even thousands, depending on the size of each family. All family members are expected to be at the Covenant Ceremony.

It is important that all family members witness this Covenant taking place, so that they can tell their children and their children can tell their children for generations and generations. All generations to come get the same benefits that are decided upon on this day of the Covenant Ceremony. The only requirement that a person from another generation has to fulfill to receive all these merging benefits from this Covenant, is *just to be born into the family.*

Next, the animal that will be used within the Covenant Ceremony is selected by the two families. Normally it would be the best ram or heifer the families had to offer for the

Covenant Ceremony. When these details are accomplished and all Conditions are decided upon and made clear to both sides of the families, the Covenant Ceremony can commence.

Chapter Three

I WILL NEVER FORGET

Genesis 15:10 (AMP) – "And he brought Him all these and cut them down the middle [into halves] and laid each half opposite the other;. . ."

e wrote earlier what "Covenant" meant in Hebrew. Let's look at that again. "Covenant" in Hebrew is *beriyth (ber-eeth');* **a compact made by passing between pieces of flesh: covenant, league. To cut, To divide.** I know that in our thinking of what the word "Covenant" means, this would not be it. Throughout this Book, I invite you to visualize the many descriptions and images that we will look at in The Word and picture what lengths God and His People went through to make and keep Blood Covenants. Allow me to continue on the ceremonial process of this extremely important trans-action between two families called Covenant and the true meaning of it. Let's go together on an intimate journey of how a Covenant actually comes into being through **The Blood Covenant Ceremony.**

Blood Covenant

Representative is Chosen
Covenant Site is Chosen
Conditions of Covenant are decided on and declared
Animal(s) is cut
Walk of Blood
Cutting of Representative's Flesh
Promises Proclaimed and Names are Combined
Giving of Coats
Trading of Belts
Covenant Meal

The Covenant Site has been selected and it's a beautiful morning and everyone in the village is spilling over with excitement, for everyone knows today is the day that the Covenant is to happen. Everyone in their respective homes will prepare themselves and their children to go to the Covenant Site, for their attendance is required today for the momentous ceremony. Family members far and wide will attend the ceremony. Many may have to travel long distances to arrive at the Covenant Site. All will make that journey. All will witness this important day in their lives and their family's future. When both families arrive in their entirety, many hugs and embraces occur, as some family members have not seen the others for quite some time. It truly is an exciting day. What is wonderful for the Covenant families is that even though only one member from each family is the Covenant Representative who goes through the Blood Covenant Ceremony that they will be observing, *family members get all the benefits that the Representative pays for in The Ceremony!* The only thing that family member has to do to receive The Full Benefits of The Blood Covenant Ceremony *is just be born into the family!*

As the set time approaches, all family members from both sides of the two Covenant families draw near. One family's crowd of members stands on one side and the other family's members on the other side–two separate crowds of people, each family facing the other family they are about to join.

The Covenant Representative then comes out from among his family. He stands in front of his family alone and begins to make his way to the center between the two families. The second family's representative leaves his family and comes to the center also. The two representatives face each other and silence comes over the two crowds behind them. Both representatives realize that they and their families will never be the same as they stand facing each other. All the families watch this history-making ceremony.

The Covenant Animal or Animals that have been selected are brought to the center of the two families, where the representatives are standing. The rams or heifers have been selected beforehand. They are the best of the families' possessions.

The Covenant Cut is performed on the Covenant Animals. The animals are split right down the spines of their bodies. The two halves of the animal are made to fall opposite each other. If two animals are used for the Covenant Ceremony, then the second animal is positioned either right in front of or right behind the other animal. In the center of the two halves of the animal(s) a natural blood flow occurs. Blood from within both sides of the animal(s) that have been cut flows to the ground between the two halves of flesh. This blood flow creates an *"alley-way"* of blood between the two halves. This *"alley-way"* will be known as the *"walkway of blood" for the representatives.*

Giving of the Coats or Robes - The two representatives are standing within the sacrificed animal's blood and innards. Each representative takes off his coat and gives it to the other representative. The coat signifies authority. For example, a military coat represents the authority and rank of a person. When the coats are exchanged the two men are saying on behalf of themselves and their families, who are all present and witnessing,

All that I am and who I am, I give to you. I give you all my authority. You may use my authority to live your life. You have my authority now and I have yours.

Trading of the Belts - Next, the belts of weapons are taken off. The girdle that is worn that carries the sword, the daggers and all the types of weaponry that the family would carry. The girdles or belts of weapons are then given from one representative to the other, both exchanging their belts or girdles that hold all of their weapons. This exchange represents that:

I give you all my strength. Your enemies are now mine. I'll fight for you even if I die. When you go to battle I will always be by your side fighting alongside you and for you and your family, even to the death.

The Walk of Blood then follows. As the two halves of the Covenant Animal(s) have been sliced, the representatives then walk between the two halves that have fallen apart and are facing each other. The blood that has drained from these animals into the center by this time is very deep. Again, the blood flow creates an "alleyway" of blood between the two halves. This "alleyway" will be known as the "walkway of blood." The representatives for the families walk through the "blood alley" twice, then they stop in the center of the two halves of the animal and face each other. They are ankle to knee deep in blood. The smell, the feeling and sight of the raw flesh, organs, guts and blood all around their <u>feet</u>, <u>ankles</u> and legs are overwhelming! Possibly the undigested food that was in the animal, now laying out of it or in the blood where they now stand, which is very difficult to bear. This is an experience that they will NEVER FORGET!

Conditions of the Covenant - While standing and facing each other in this pool of blood and animal entrails, the two representatives then say to each other on behalf of themselves and the families:

*Even as I stand here in the midst of this animal's death,
I will stand with you in the midst of death. This is forever.
I will stand with you. I cannot and will not ever break my
promise and Covenant with you.*

Promises Proclaimed - Then the two representatives, while still standing and facing each other in between the animals, speak out loud all the promises that the families decided on in the Covenant Negotiations. All the families present hear the promises that are being made to the other family. These vows are specifically spoken to the other and promised to be carried out by both families. Next, the representatives speak out loud that they swear by the blessings and promises of God that they will fulfill their promises. This makes God the third witness to the Covenant that is taking place between the two families on this very special day.

The Cutting of the Flesh is the next step of this Covenant Ceremony. While the Covenant representatives are standing in the pool of blood around their ankles and legs and the two families are taking part in the service, the Cutting of The Flesh is to be done. The two representatives will now make an incision on their body. Normally it was on either the hand or wrist.

Blood would begin to flow out of their own bodies. The two family's blood was now being shed. The hands or wrists of the two representatives would come together by either holding their wrists up in the air together or joining their hands together up in the air. With hands lifted, their blood flowing down their arms, joining together and mingling together their blood, they state by words and action that:

I, as the chosen representative on behalf of my family, promise to uphold this Covenant with your family! I will and so will my family, so help me God!

The scars of these incisions on the representative's arms or wrists are the seals of the Covenant. The scars will never go away, just like the promises made this day are to never go away.

The Names of the Two Families Are Combined while the two representatives are still standing within the center of the Covenant Animal's remains. Both representatives shout out loud for all to hear the New Names that have been decided upon before the Blood Covenant Ceremony began. The merged names of the families are for the first time spoken and are now officially changed within the two families.

The Covenant Meal is the last part of this Blood Covenant Ceremony. The two representatives of the families, the leaders and all the family members have a Covenant Meal together. The most important items of this Covenant Meal are the bread and the wine. When the bread is eaten by the two Covenant families it represents to each other that:

Now that we are in Blood Covenant with each other, I would eat my own flesh before I would let you die! You will never be alone again!

And when the wine is drunk by the two Covenant families it is representing to the other family that:

This wine is like the blood of my body. My blood is my life. As we drink this wine together, my life is now your life.

The bread and the wine are the final fulfillment of the terms of the Blood Covenant Ceremony. The two families are now one. . . forever!

Telling The Story

Forever, the two representatives and their families will recall this day. Their responsibility is to tell others for generations to come about his or her experience on this day of Covenant. The representatives and the families of the Covenant with all their hearts will remember this day and what they gave up and what they received. This Covenant is so deep that it will always be on the representatives' and the families' minds. You can hear the representatives sharing their memories with the ones that were to follow them:

> *As I look upon the scar on my own body, I recall our Covenant with you. You are constantly on my mind, you are ever before me. I live in constant memory of my promises to you and shall keep them before me. It's as if I'm standing in the blood of the Covenant Ceremony making my commitments to you right now. Though many years ago, it is still so fresh and real in my memory and will always be. I can still feel the blood up to my ankles. I still can remember the smell of the insides of the animal I stood in, and feel the warmth of it all around my legs and feet. I constantly recollect my own blood flowing down my body from the Covenant Cut I made. Look here at the scar of Covenant that we have with them. As this scar is forever, our promises are forever. And I will forever remember them.*

And as for the family members who witnessed this history-changing day, they will never forget the sights, the smells, the seriousness and the rejoicing that it brought to them and their families. You might hear them recall it like this:

> *I'll never forget it. Seeing all my distant family all gathering, all standing together, people that we are about to be joined with. I remember the Conditions of The Covenant being shouted out by the Leaders so we could hear it. And oh, how sweet they were to all of our ears! They are strong in battle and in might and they win in every war. This family that we joined with was promising to never leave us, to help us when we needed it, to fight with us in war, to be with us and for us. . . forever! I remember their Covenant Representative and ours both*

standing in that pool of blood together. I saw the blood, I smelled the blood, and heard it all that day. I witnessed the Trading of the Belts and Robes in the blood. . . oh my child, I tell you these things so that you will tell your children and their children will tell their children. . . that you are never alone and we as a family are never alone! For we are in a Blood Covenant relationship with this wonderful other family! And what was joined was not just for that day, or even for just us who witnessed it. No, my child, it was done for you and all the generations of our family to come!

Yes, those initial family members that were present during that Blood Covenant Ceremony that day have a responsibility to tell the next generation of the Covenant that now includes them! Then that following generation has the obligation to tell the next generation and so on. This Blood Covenant that was cut is FOREVER! And ALL that is born into either of the two families that were joined in the Blood Covenant from now on are STILL and WILL ALWAYS BE joined to each other! Telling the Conditions of The Covenant that was Cut with the families to come is crucial for the continuing generations. Everyone must know what they possess with the Covenant Family they are forever joined with! Amazing!

Chapter Four

HOW WILL I KNOW?

*"But he [Abram] said, Lord God, by what shall I know
that I shall inherit it?"* Genesis 15:8 (AMP)

*W*hat does God think about Covenants and how seri-
ously does He take them? Let's look at one of God's
Covenants in the Old Testament. God needed to find a man
on earth to make a Covenant with to bless his family, for man
had fallen in the Garden of Eden through Adam. Abram (later
Abraham) was the man. In Genesis chapter 14 we see how
Abram went after the ones who had captured his nephew, Lot.
He was victorious and brought back Lot, all the goods, his possessions, the women and the people captured. Abram gave
Melchizedek, the priest of God, a tenth of all he had taken.
Then Abram declared that he wouldn't be taking for himself
any of the goods, so that the king of Sodom couldn't say that
he had made Abram rich. In chapter 15, verse 1 (AMP), we
see God telling Abram after all of this:

> *"After these things, the word of the Lord came to Abram
> in a vision, saying, Fear not, Abram, I am your Shield
> (King), your abundant compensation, and your reward
> shall be exceedingly great."* ("King" written in by writer,
> "Shield" also meaning "King" here. See Amplified
> Translation Footnote.)

God begins to tell Abram that He, not man, will compensate and reward him. Abram decided not to take the spoils from a man, so God reassured Abram that He would *reward and compensate* him. He tells Abram that He is his King and will provide greatly for him in possessions. He also tells Abram that He is going to make his descendants as numerous as the stars, even though Abram is older and so is Sarai (Abram's wife). Sarai is also barren and had never had children. (Genesis 15:1-5)

Distant Shores Media/Sweet Publishing

We find that Abram believed what God was telling him, for in verse 6 it shows us, *"And he [Abram] believed in (trusted in, relied on, remained steadfast to) the Lord, and He counted it to him as righteousness (right standing with God)."* Then when we arrive at verse 8 we see that Abram asks God a question: *"Lord, God, by what shall I <u>know</u> that I shall inherit it?"* Abram believed in and trusted in what God was telling him (verse 6), he just needed a deeper knowing within himself to hold on to about what God was saying to him. The word "know" here in verse 8 is the word *yada' (yaw-dah')*. It is the same word that is used in Genesis 4:1:

> *"And Adam <u>knew</u> Eve as his wife, and she became pregnant and bore Cain; and she said, I have gotten and gained a man with the help of the Lord."*

Yada' has various deep meanings. God told Abram that He would be his Shield, Compensation, and Reward. Abram believed God's Words to him and what He spoke. Abram now was requesting in verse 8 to "yada", to "know," by a deep encounter or experience what God was promising to him. Abram desired an experience that would enable him to "yada" and to unite and be as one with God. Abram sought God to give him something that he could know, or "yada," to completely be like-minded and totally give his desires, present, future, trust, family, provisions and even his own body to. That's what God did. He gave Abram a Covenant.

Remember all that we have learned about Covenant in the previous section of this book. We will clearly be able to see what God Himself was doing with man. If you are like me, I've read these scriptures so many times and did not really know what was truly happening here. Let's look at this together. We find in Genesis 15:8-18 (NIV):

> *"But Abram said, "O Sovereign LORD, how can I know that I will gain possession of it?" 9 So the LORD said to him, "Bring me a heifer, a goat and a ram, each three*

years old, along with a dove and a young pigeon." 10 Abram brought all these to him, cut them in two and arranged the halves opposite each other; the birds, however, he did not cut in half.. . . 12 As the sun was setting, Abram fell into a deep sleep, and a thick and dreadful darkness came over him. . . 17 When the sun had set and darkness had fallen, a smoking firepot with a blazing torch appeared and passed between the pieces. 18 On that day the LORD made **a covenant** *with Abram and said, "To your descendants I give this land, from the river of Egypt to the great river, the Euphrates. . ."*

God Himself decided to give Abram the deepest and most solemn thing he could do – He Cut a Covenant with man that day. The word "covenant" in verse 18 is the same Hebrew word *beriyth (ber-eeth')* OT:1285. Remember, *beriyth (ber-eeth')* means **a compact made by passing between pieces of flesh: covenant, league. To cut. To divide.** The Bible is letting us know that there was a Covenant Ceremony taking place. The Covenant Site was chosen. The Conditions of the Covenant were spoken out loud. The Representatives were chosen; in this case, it was God and Abram. The animals were selected by Abram and God. A heifer, a goat, a ram (all three years old), a dove and a pigeon were the animals chosen for this Covenant Ceremony.

Abram prepared the Covenant Animals by *cutting them in half and the halves of flesh lay opposite each other.* The birds were sacrificed but not cut in half for the Covenant Ceremony. God allowed Abram to go into a deep sleep, where he gave him the truths about his descendants' future and what God promised to do. God *Himself,* The Representative of the Covenant, came in the form of "a smoking firepot with a blazing torch." God as one of the Covenant Representatives "walked" or "passed" through the middle of the Covenant Animals. Keep in mind, *beriyth (ber-eeth')* means **a compact made by passing between pieces of flesh: covenant, league. To cut. To divide.**

*"When the sun had set and darkness had fallen, a smoking firepot with a blazing torch appeared and passed between the pieces. On that day the LORD made **a covenant** with Abram. . ."* (Genesis 15:17-18 (NIV))

God was The One Who committed the Walk of Blood in the Covenant Ceremony, while Abram made the Covenant Cut on the Covenant Animals.

Distant Shores Media/Sweet Publishing

God, Himself

Can you imagine this picture? There, lying on the ground, are these Covenant Animals that have been cut in half, their blood and insides running into the middle of this fleshy valley and God Himself is making His way through the center of the walls of the slaughtered animals as a smoking firepot with a blazing torch in the darkness of the night – all to make Promises and Covenant with Abram and all his descendants! Why? Because God is serious about His Promises, His Word and His Covenants!

Later, Exodus 13:22 (AMP) shows us how God appeared to His People, the descendants that God promised Abram he would have. (*"The pillar of cloud by day and the pillar of fire by night did not depart from before the people."*) God, Who in the future with Abram's descendants (Moses, Aaron and all the Hebrew Children that came out of Egypt) that He prophesied to Abram about, guided them and was with them. God showed Himself to them as a "fire by night and a cloud by day."

God was even showing His appearance, as it would be with Moses and the Hebrew Children many years in the future, to Abram that night during the Covenant Ceremony as a "smoking (a cloud) firepot and a blazing (fire) torch." He showed Abram He was and would be with him and his descendants as smoke (or cloud) and fire. Isn't it marvelous, that as Father God was partaking in His part of the Covenant Ceremony with Abram, He manifested Himself in a form that would be exemplary of how He would make Himself apparent to Abram's descendants (Moses and the Hebrew Children) later in history!

God is so faithful to His Covenant, His People and His Ways. And because of *this* Blood Covenant Ceremony, Israel would begin her matrimonial relationship with Father God, Her Husband.

Chapter Five

WHILE YOU WERE SLEEPING

🌰

". . . a deep sleep to fall upon Adam; and while he
slept. . ." Genesis 2: 21 (AMP)

𝒩 ow, that we've addressed Abraham and his Blood
Covenant Ceremony with Father God, let's look at The
Very FIRST Covenant that God cut with the man named Adam.
This is where God Himself decided to come into <u>Covenant</u>
or <u>Marry</u> <u>Mankind</u>! *That's just amazing to think about, isn't*
it? We talked about the Blood Covenant Ceremony between
Abraham and God first, for it is very demonstrative of the process that takes place within The Blood Covenant Ceremony.
The Blood Covenant with Abraham, though very different than
the Covenant Ceremony that was cut with Adam, did have a
few similarities.

"And Adam gave names to all the livestock and to the
birds of the air and to every [wild] beast of the field; but
for Adam there was not found a helper meet (suitable,
adapted, complementary) for him. 21 And the Lord God
caused a deep sleep to fall upon Adam; and while he
slept, He took one of his ribs or a part of his side and
closed up the [place with] flesh. 22 And the rib or part
of his side which the Lord God had taken from the man

He built up and made into a woman, and He brought her to the man.

23 Then Adam said, This [creature] is now bone of my bones and flesh of my flesh; she shall be called Woman, because she was taken out of a man. 24 Therefore a man shall leave his father and his mother and shall become united and cleave to his wife, and they shall become one flesh. 25 And the man and his wife were both naked and were not embarrassed or ashamed in each other's presence." Genesis 2:20-25 (AMP)

Distant Shores Media/Sweet Publishing

The Covenant Site was determined by God as the Garden of Eden. The two Covenant Representatives in this Blood Covenant Ceremony were Adam and Father God, one man and God. In the Blood Covenant with Abraham and Father God, there were just two, Abram, (later Abraham) a man, and God. And much like the Covenant Ceremony that occurred between Abram and God, Adam was put into a *deep sleep* and so was the Covenant Representative Abram. Both times the man in the Blood Covenant Ceremony has to be put in a sleep, for God Himself was present! Hallelujah! And also we should point out that *Adam* and *Abram's* names are almost spelled alike.

The Beauty of the Side

No "livestock" animal would be used as the Covenant Animal to be Cut in this Ceremony between Adam and God. No, God determined to create a "creature" or "creation" like Him and like Adam. He used Adam, the one He wanted to have Covenant with as the "creature" to be Cut for Covenant. Adam was put into a deep sleep so that God could make a "holy incision" in Adam's **side** (remember, the Covenant Animals are always cut down the center or side of their bodies!) God took one of Adam's ribs, or a part of his side, and then closed the opening with flesh. The Covenant Cut was made on the Covenant "animal" or "creature" or "creation", Adam.

The Covenant Cut was made on Adam by God. So where was the blood that was needed to make this a Blood Covenant Ceremony between the two? The blood was in the bone or rib that was taken out by God Himself! The bones in our bodies are so amazing. They function to move, support, and protect the various organs of our bodies; **they also produce red and white blood cells and store minerals. There are blood vessels in the marrow inside our bones. The bone marrow inside our bones produces the blood that is then sent through tiny holes in our bones throughout our bodies.**

There is also plasma in blood, and it is mostly water (90% by volume).

When God took that bone out of Adam to make "Woman", there was a blood sacrifice made **from the side** of the "Covenant Animal or Creature (Adam)" through Adam's bone. The bone taken out of Adam's body had within it **blood.** Remember, the bone marrow within that bone would have created blood inside of it to be sent out into his body. The blood within that bone taken from Adam's side could be lawfully used by God to complete the Blood Covenant procedure.

Also, we noted that plasma, which is mostly water (90% by volume), is within blood, which is produced in our bones. **The First Adam had blood and water through his bone come out of his side to birth his Bride, "Woman" and The Last Adam, Jesus, had blood and water flow from His side birthing His Bride, The Church!**

"But one of the soldiers pierced <u>His side</u> with a spear, and immediately <u>blood</u> and <u>water</u> came (flowed) out." John 19:34 (AMP))

And out of that flow of blood and water came Jesus' Bride, The Church! God used an "incision" on the First Adam's side to get a bone with blood and water in it to deliver his bride, "Woman." And from The Last Adam's Side, the blood and water in Him came out by the spear to His Side to birth His Bride. . . and when women deliver mankind out of them today, blood and water usher the birth of yet another addition to mankind! "Woman" was "born" from the blood and water of Adam. The Bride of Christ was born out of Jesus' Water and Blood. We are born once in the Natural way and then we are to be Born Again through Jesus! Both Adams are used to Birth! The first experience of birth, we have no control over, the second we do!

The Last Adam, Jesus, gave of His Body, His Blood, His Water, Himself for The Bride of Christ to be birthed, as did the First Adam with his bride "Woman." We, The Church and

Jesus' Bride, began from inside His Body. In Galatians 3:19, Jesus is called *The Seed.*

What does a "seed" have in it? Although you can't see it from the outside, inside a "seed" is a tree. And on that tree are, let's say, apples. And within those apples are more seeds and apples to come. And within all those apples, the seeds could be planted and then you would have an orchard of apples. The entire orchard was within the first seed. And all that Jesus, The Seed, paid for was within Him, just like a "seed" in the natural world must "die" first before what's in it comes out!

> *"I assure you, most solemnly I tell you, Unless a grain of wheat falls into the earth and dies, it remains [just one grain; it never becomes more but lives] by itself alone. But if it dies, it produces many others and yields a rich harvest."* John 12:24 (AMP)

Jesus, The Seed, had to die so that what was within Him for US would come out! Jesus used His Precious Body as the Container that carried The Blood, the Water, the sin of all mankind, all pain, sickness, despair, curses. . . everything was paid for with His Body, and it was all to birth His Bride!

We, The Church, came from The Last Adam's Side, just like "Woman" came from Adam's side. Remember, the bone of Adam's side had within it blood and water. And God took that sacrifice and gave him a bride, just like He gave Jesus one! Why did all of this have to happen to both The First Adam and The Last Adam, Jesus, and why did blood have to come from them in this manner? Because The Covenant Animal had to have a Covenant Cut in the side and blood had to come from that side according to The Blood Covenant Ceremony. And it did in the First Adam and The Last Adam, Jesus! Both had blood *and water* come from them to pay for and to birth their Brides!

While Asleep

And if that's not wonderful enough, in both the First Adam and The Last Adam's sacrifice, both were "asleep!" Adam was put into a deep sleep so that he could have the Covenant Cut of The Blood Covenant Ceremony made by God on his side and the blood and water could come out to birth his bride through his bone. And The Last Adam, Jesus, was in a place of being "asleep" when The Covenant Cut was made on His Side so that The Blood and Water could birth His Bride, The Church!

"But when they came to Jesus and found that he was already dead*, they did not break his legs. 34 Instead, one of the soldiers* pierced Jesus' side *with a spear,* **bringing a sudden flow of blood and water."** (John 19:33-34 (NIV))

Many times in The Word of God "death" is referred to as simply "being asleep." One example of this is when Jesus was talking about Lazarus being "asleep."

"He said these things, and then added, Our friend Lazarus *is at* rest and sleeping*; but I am going there that I may awaken him out of his sleep. 12 The disciples answered, Lord, if he is sleeping, he will recover. 13 However, Jesus had spoken of* his death*, but they thought that He referred to falling into a refreshing and natural sleep. 14 So then Jesus told them plainly,* Lazarus is dead*,"* John 11:11-14 (AMP)

Jesus, The Last Adam, was "dead" or "asleep" when The Covenant Cut was made in His Side and Blood flowed out of that Side and Water flowed, birthing His Bride, The Church, just like the first Adam was asleep when The Covenant Cut was made on him. How amazing is that? How meticulous our God is in fulfilling His Blood Covenant Conditions with God and with us! The Blood Covenant Ceremony had to be fulfilled for us to come into Covenant with God, and Jesus did it to the fullest! *(The greater details of Jesus' Blood Covenant Ceremony will be later within this Book.)*

Covenant Conditions – Even Then

When Adam awoke and perceived the wonder and beauty of this new creature called Woman, Covenant Conditions of The Blood Covenant Ceremony were stated out loud by one of the Covenant Representatives, Adam:

"*Then Adam said, This [creature]. . .*

(Remember Adam is talking about Woman as the "creature" here.)

. . . is now bone of my bones and flesh of my flesh; she shall be called Woman, because she was taken out of a man. 24 Therefore a man shall leave his father and his mother and shall become united and cleave to his wife, and they shall become one flesh." Genesis 2:23-24 (AMP)

Even though Adam was asleep, he declared when he awoke that the bone that had come from him was "Woman's" now too. He was saying out loud a true element of The Blood Covenant Ceremony. Adam was fulfilling The Covenant Conditions, as if to say :

All that I am and all that I have is yours. You are now a part of me, you are a part of my family and I a part of yours. Our lives, being and future are as one flesh; we are a family together.

My Name Is Yours

Another part of the Blood Covenant Ceremony that took place is the declaring of the Covenant New Names. As we have seen earlier in this book, the Covenant Representative declares that the two persons or families that are merging change their names to show that they are now as one. Adam, or "Man", declared that this one that has come from his bone and flesh is one with him and is called "WoMAN!"

What happened here between Adam, or "Man", and "Woman" is just as if two families had come together in a Covenant Ceremony and their names are combined. Remember The Smith family and the Jones family example given earlier? During the Blood Covenant Ceremony the Smithjones family or the Jonesmith family's Names were combined. Adam took his identity of "Man" (which is one of the things Adam means) and gave this new creature his name, "Man" also. Then he added her name or identity to his as "Man": a "Man with a Womb", making her "Woman" and therefore fulfilling The Blood Covenant Ceremony's part called Declaring and Merging of The Covenant New Names.

The two had merged. The Blood Covenant was cut from the side of the Covenant "Animal" Adam, the new names were given, and a marriage or Covenant had been brought together that day through Adam, God and "Woman." Though Adam may not have known at that very moment that he was following Covenant Ceremony Protocol, God knew, because God is faithful to His Covenant and always shall be.

This Is Just Amazing, God!

What we see here is simply amazing! On the Covenant day that God, Man and Woman came together, we see Adam prophetically stating many declarations of the Covenant Conditions. We've read about Genesis 2:23-24. Let's look at it one more time.

*"Then Adam said, **This** [creature] is now bone of my bones and flesh of my flesh; she shall be called **Woman**, because **she was taken out of a man**. 24 Therefore **a man shall leave his father and his mother and shall become united and cleave to his wife**, and they shall become one flesh."* Genesis 2:23-24 (AMP)

First, in verse 23 we see the word "This." When one looks up the Hebrew meaning of this word we find the word *zo'th (zothe')* OT:2063. It shows us that the Hebrew word OT:2063 (Hebrew and Greek words in The Word of God have numbers that help you in your research of what the words mean in your Bible) comes from the "irregular feminine" root word of OT:2089.

I know that sounds like a lot, but basically it means that. . . OT:2089 is *(zeh)* which means a **sheep** or **lamb.** Adam was calling the new man with a womb (Woman) also a <u>lamb</u> or <u>sheep</u> when He was speaking in verse 23. He actually was saying:

"This" or **(the lamb or sheep)** *creature is now bone of my bones and flesh of my flesh. . ."*

Adam was calling himself a *lamb or* sheep (since that's what "This" - OT: 2089 means) and stating that this new crea-ture called Woman was one too, since Woman came from him. Adam said that Woman was his flesh and bone, so she came from him. So that would make **Adam** a <u>lamb</u> or <u>sheep,</u> too!

Could this have been the beginning of The First Adam (or first lamb or sheep) identifying himself prophetically with The Last Adam, Jesus, The Lamb of God? Adam, by calling Woman a "lamb", was seeing that this new "creature", "Woman", would be used to bring forth many "sheep" to eventually birth The Lamb of God, Jesus!

Many "sheep" would be birthed through being Born Again into The Kingdom of God through Jesus The Christ, just like many "sheep" would be birthed from this creature called Woman! So, when Adam was identifying Woman (Man with a womb) to also be a "lamb" or "sheep," Adam was calling forth who she was and what Woman would birth in the natural way, which is many other "sheep."

And yet Adam was prophetically calling forth what this "lamb," Woman, would be used to birth, and that would eventually be The "Lamb" of God! Remember, Jesus calls us sheep. We become sheep, His sheep, when we are saved. We come from The "Lamb," Jesus! We are "birthed" or re-born through Him! Many "sheep" have come from Him, too! And we are to follow Him as sheep! So it makes perfect sense that prophetically Adam was calling out that a "lamb" or "sheep" came out of him, which was Woman. And that's why Jesus calls us "sheep", too!

*"My **sheep** hear my voice, and I know them, and they follow me:" John 10:27 (KJV)*

We, as "sheep" or "lambs", are birthed in the natural way and that all started in the Garden of Eden from the first "lamb" or "sheep", Adam and Eve (Woman.) And then if we give our lives to Jesus, we are then birthed again from The Lamb and join the multitude of His Sheep. God used Adam to speak our identities today, Woman's then and even Jesus' to come as the "lambs" and "sheep" of The Family of God. Jesus is called The Last Adam and The Lamb of God!

The First Covenant Animal

The "Covenant Animal" (Adam) was the first *"lamb"* that was "Cut" so that another could live! **As Jesus was and is The Last Adam and The Lamb of God, He would do the same and be "Cut" so that others may live!** *The First Adam was the Covenant Animal that was Cut in that First Covenant Ceremony in the Garden of Eden and so the Last Adam, Jesus, The Christ, was the Covenant Animal to be Cut in His Covenant Ceremony!* Jesus is called The Lamb of God and The Last Adam, because the first Adam (Man) was also a lamb!

There would never be a need for another descendant of Adam (Man) to retrieve all that we lost in the beginning in the Garden of Eden. The Last Adam, Jesus, took care of it all. And there would never need to be another need for a lamb (OT:2089 (*zeh*)) to be "Cut" so another could live. The Lamb of God took the care of that, too!

Adam continued to declare the Covenant Conditions in the Garden: "This [creature]" was a Woman (man with womb) and that "she was taken out of man." For, as <u>she</u> was taken out of man, <u>man</u> or <u>mankind</u> would be taken or come from this new creature called Woman. This new man had a womb to birth man from. Then Adam continues to proclaim that:

". . . a man shall leave his father and his mother and shall become united and cleave to his wife. . ."

There were no fathers and mothers at this time! Adam and Woman were the first people in the Garden, so how did Adam know what a father or mother was? And then Adam speaks over the Woman yet another identity and that is, she is *his wife!*

How could he even know what a "wife" was or for that matter, what a womb was? Again, Adam was prophetically announcing truths that only God could have given him— Covenant Truths and Conditions at the Covenant Ceremony between the Representatives, God The Father, The Son, The Holy Spirit, Adam and Woman.

"God said, Let <u>Us</u> [Father, Son, and Holy Spirit] make mankind in Our image, after Our likeness, and let them have complete authority over the fish of the sea, the birds of the air, the [tame] beasts, and over all of the earth, and over everything that creeps upon the earth." Gen. 1:26 (AMP)

God also made Covenant Conditions at this Covenant Ceremony. (Genesis 1:26-30 (AMP) reads:

"God said, Let Us [Father, Son, and Holy Spirit] make mankind in Our image, after Our likeness, and let them have complete authority over the fish of the sea, the birds of the air, the [tame] beasts, and over all of the earth, and over everything that creeps upon the earth. 27 So God created man in His own image, in the image and likeness of God He created him; male and female He created them. 28 And God blessed them and said to them, Be fruitful, multiply, and fill the earth, and subdue it [using all its vast resources in the service of God and man]; and have dominion over the fish of the sea, the birds of the air, and over every living creature that moves upon the earth.

29 And God said, See, I have given you every plant yielding seed that is on the face of all the land and every tree with seed in its fruit; you shall have them for food. 30 And to all the animals on the earth and to every bird of the air and to everything that creeps on the ground–to everything in which there is the breath of life–I have given every green plant for food. And it was so."

Father God, the Son and The Holy Spirit were very much The Representatives stating The Conditions of The Covenant that day with Man and Woman, for they had everything to offer and give. The other Representatives (Adam and Eve) had everything to <u>receive</u> and yet Adam and Eve's part was to carry out and fulfill what was given to them during the Covenant Ceremony that day. And they did carry out their terms of The Covenant, until they chose to break their side of the Covenant and surrender to another – God's enemy!

God, then found another man to reestablish this Covenant with: Abram, later to be named Abraham. God got this man, Abram to agree to be in Covenant with Him and with the Promises, for Abram and his future family. Let's look at that future family.

Chapter Six

SHOW ME YOUR GLORY

*"Now if you obey me fully and keep my covenant, then
out of all nations you will be my treasured possession."*
Exodus 19: 5 (NIV)

So let's look at the ones that were specifically mentioned
within Abram's Blood Covenant Ceremony, for this group
of People would in the future be carrying out those Covenant
Conditions. Remember that when a Covenant is cut, the
future family members receive the Covenant Promises, too!

And when did God declare that there would be others
in the future? God tells us about the ones that He will next
cut Covenant with at the Covenant Ceremony that God has
with Abraham (see Genesis 15)! Right when the Covenant
Ceremony is taking place with Abraham and God is within
those halves of flesh and blood in the animals, God speaks
as one of the Conditions of Covenant that He will take care of
the future family of Abraham, which is exactly what happens
when you come into Blood Covenant with another family: You
fight in battles, bring aid and rescue the other family!

*"And [God] said to Abram, Know positively that your
descendants will be strangers dwelling as temporary
residents in a land that is not theirs [Egypt], and they
will be slaves there and will be afflicted and oppressed*

for 400 years. [Fulfilled in Exodus 12:40.]" 14 But I will bring judgment on that nation whom they will serve, and afterward they will come out with great possessions." Genesis 15:13-14 (AMP)

So the descendants of Abraham that God is talking about here are the Hebrew Children that were slaves in Egypt that Moses would lead! And yes, just like verse 14 states, much "judgment" was displayed in Egypt before Pharaoh would release Abraham's family. There were great plagues of blood, frogs, gnats, a plague on livestock, boils, hail, locusts, darkness and the plague on the firstborn. All of these happened to the Nation of Egypt, who would not allow God's People (Abraham's family) to leave. These People were slaves in Egypt, but that didn't cancel The Blood Covenant that Father God had cut with Abraham! And because of that Blood Covenant, God blessed and rescued Abraham's family out of Egypt! God is serious about His Promises and His Covenant! And He *never* forgets the Conditions of Covenant, not for a hundred or a thousand years from making them. . . *He never forgets!*

And As You Go. . .

The other thing that stands out in Genesis 15:14 is that God says during the Blood Covenant Ceremony with Abraham that Abraham's family that were in Egypt and slaves would come out of Egypt with great possessions! Pharaoh leads the Egyptians in telling Moses after all those plagues:

"Take your flocks and herds, as you said, and be gone. Go, but bless me as you leave." 33 All the Egyptians urged the people of Israel to get out of the land as quickly as possible, for they thought, "We will all die!"

34 The Israelites took their bread dough before yeast was added. They wrapped their kneading boards in

their cloaks and carried them on their shoulders. 35
And the people of Israel did as Moses had instructed;
they asked the Egyptians for clothing and articles of
silver and gold. 36 The LORD caused the Egyptians
to look favorably on the Israelites, and they gave the
Israelites whatever they asked for. **So they stripped**
the Egyptians of their wealth!

37 That night the people of Israel left Rameses and
started for Succoth. There were about 600,000 men,
plus all the women and children. 38 A rabble of non-
Israelites went with them, along with great flocks and
herds of livestock." Exodus 12:32-38 (NLT)

The people of Egypt gave Abraham's family what they
asked them for! And just like Father God said as one of
The Conditions of Covenant in Abraham's Blood Covenant
Ceremony, Abraham's family would come out of a bad situation with great possessions – *"But I will bring judgment on that*
nation whom they will serve, and afterward they will come out
with great possessions."

Yes, when two families join in Blood Covenant, there is
help, aid, fighting with the other in war and there is *provision!*
For when both of the families join together, one shares with
the other! God is absolutely rich and when He came into Blood
Covenant with Abraham, He blessed him financially and here
we see The Covenant working again and again. Abraham's
family (the Hebrew Children in Egypt) was a part of that Blood
Covenant just by being in the family of Abraham. Abraham
had never met them, nor they Abraham! And because of that
Blood Covenant Ceremony and because Father God was
the other Family Abraham was joined with, those Hebrew
Children leaving Egypt received wealth from the other in this
Covenant. . . Father God!

God used the Egyptians to bring wealth to Abraham's
family. And since The Blood Covenant Ceremony Abraham
and Father God had joined in together, Abraham's family

is now God's family! And Abraham's family included those Hebrew Children in Egypt years later! And again, God is rich! He doesn't mind using gold to pave His streets! So He Who Abraham had come into Covenant with also brought his family into Covenant with him. . . And Who is the richest Person ever? Father God, Himself! And that's Who Abraham and his family were then and forever more in Covenant with!

How'd We Get There?

Now, what's even more Good News is that WE now are a part of Abraham's family too!

"The real children of Abraham, then, are those who put their faith in God. 8 What's more, the Scriptures looked forward to this time when God would declare the Gentiles to be righteous because of their faith. God proclaimed this good news to Abraham long ago when he said, "All nations will be blessed through you."

9 So all who put their faith in Christ share the same blessing Abraham received because of his faith.. . . 17 Through Christ Jesus, God has blessed the Gentiles with the same blessing he promised to Abraham, so that we who are believers might receive the promised Holy Spirit through faith." Galatians 3:7-9,17 (NLT)

The Bible says that, *"Through Christ Jesus"* we get the *"same blessing he promised to Abraham."* Now, HOW did WE get to be a part of Abraham's family, if we are not Hebrew or an Israelite or Jewish? The Bible tells us that we've been grafted or, if you will, "inserted" into all of this wonderful Covenant and family of Abraham and Father God! We are specifically told:

"Therefore, remember that at one time you were Gentiles (heathens) in the flesh, called Uncircumcision

by those who called themselves Circumcision, [itself a mere mark] in the flesh made by human hands. 12 [Remember] that you were at that time separated (living apart) from Christ [excluded from all part in Him], <u>utterly estranged and outlawed from the rights of Israel as a nation</u>, and <u>strangers with no share in the sacred compacts of the [Messianic] promise [with no knowledge of or right in God's agreements, His covenants]</u>. And you had no hope (no promise); you were in the world without God.

*13 <u>But now in Christ Jesus</u>, you who once were [so] far away, through (by, in) the blood of Christ have been brought near. 14 For He is [Himself] our peace (our bond of unity and harmony). **He has made us both [Jew and Gentile] one [body], and has broken down (destroyed, abolished) the hostile dividing wall between us,** 15 By abolishing in His [own crucified] flesh the enmity [caused by] the Law with its decrees and ordinances [which He annulled]; that He from the two might create in Himself one new man [one new quality of humanity out of the two], so making peace. 16 And [He designed] <u>to reconcile to God both</u> **[Jew and Gentile, united] in a single body by means of His cross,** thereby killing the mutual enmity and bringing the feud to an end." Ephesians 2:11-16 (AMP)*

So, HOW did we come into The Blood Covenant that was cut between Abraham and Father God? Through Jesus and what He did! Jesus was Father God's First Born and in the Line of David, Israel's King, whose father was Jesse from *Bethlehem (where Jesus was born)*. King David was the King of *Judah* and later the other tribes made him their King of Israel. *(Jesus is The Lion of The Tribe of Judah!)*

The Tribe of Judah comes from one of Jacob's sons. Jacob's father was Isaac. Isaac's father was **Abraham,** who is where all of this came from in The Blood Covenant Ceremony!

Because Jesus was from The Family of Father God AND in the family of David on back to Abraham, He was and is <u>The Only One</u> Who could bring us into the Israelites or the Jews!

"He has made us both [Jew and Gentile] one [body], and has broken down (destroyed, abolished) the hostile dividing wall between us,. . . 16 And [He designed] <u>to reconcile to God both</u> [Jew and Gentile, united] in a single body by means of His cross,"

Before Jesus, we had no rights to and <u>"no share in the sacred compacts of the [Messianic] promise [with no knowledge of or right in God's agreements, **His covenants**]</u>. We could not be and were not a part of The Covenants of God in history, until One Person Who could link us to Israel and Israel to us, and that wonderful Person was Jesus of Nazareth, born in Bethlehem, from The Tribe of Judah!

Building and Building

We see yet another Covenant Ceremony in The Word of God that clearly shows us that God has always cut Covenant with His People and He is still keeping His Promises! Hallelujah! This next Covenant is cut with Moses and the Hebrew Children. Remember, this is the family that God told Abraham would be in slavery over 400 years, and God talked about these family members while in the midst of The Blood Covenant Ceremony He was having with Abraham!

Now, The Covenant Conditions that God had already told Abraham He would fulfill would <u>not</u> go away; remember, Covenants are forever! And this is just another picture of how Good our God is. God is shown here even now **building on top of** The Conditions of The Covenant that He has with Abraham and his descendants (his family in the future.) Yes, God decides to <u>build</u> the Covenant "Package" with the descendants of Abraham that He told Abraham would be in the future. Let's explain it like this:

> *"To speak in terms of human relations, brethren, [if] even a man makes a last will and testament (a merely human covenant), no one sets it aside or makes it void or adds to it when once it has been drawn up and signed (ratified, confirmed)."* Galatians 3:15 (AMP)

For example, let's say that you have a relative who decides to give into your life. He writes up a contract (Covenant) called a Last Will and Testament (*"Testament" means "Covenant"*). All of the legalities are done and the contract signed and it is established. All the benefits that are listed from that relative are promised to you in that Will and Testament (Covenant.) Now, if you have *another relative* who decides that they are going to bless you and give to you also and they draw up a contract or Will and Testament (Covenant) and everything is legalized and signed, that doesn't cancel out or void what the *first relative* is giving you, does it? Of course not!

But what both Wills and Testaments (Covenants) do is **add to you–and add to what you receive!** Your inheritance just got larger and was built on by the second relative! Abraham *(our relative and Father of our faith)* came into Blood Covenant with God. And because of what Jesus did and Who He Is, we are now family with God and Abraham. Now, we are going to see that the family of Abraham, the Hebrew Children, got to cut a Covenant with Father God, too! So even MORE was added to the family of Abraham! I guess you could say Abraham would be similar to *the first relative* in the Will and Testament example given above and Moses and the Hebrew Children are *the second relative!* And remember, because of Jesus, we are a part of it all!

Let's look at the Hebrew Children that were led by God and a man named Moses and their experience with Covenant.

The Covenant Site Is Chosen The Word shows us completely the very Covenant Site of this special Blood Covenant Ceremony. *"On the first day of the third month after the Israelites left Egypt—on that very day—they came to the Desert of Sinai." Exodus 19:1 (NIV)*

"The LORD said to Moses, "I am going to come to you in a dense cloud, so that the people will hear me speaking with you and will always put their trust in you." Then Moses told the LORD what the people had said. 10 And the LORD said to Moses, "Go to the people and consecrate them today and tomorrow. Have them wash their clothes 11 and be ready by the third day, <u>because on that day the LORD will come down on Mount Sinai in the sight of all the people</u>.

12 Put limits for the people around the mountain and tell them, 'Be careful that you do not approach the mountain or touch the foot of it. Whoever touches the mountain is to be put to death. 13 They are to be stoned or shot with arrows; not a hand is to be laid on them. No person or animal shall be permitted to live.' Only when the ram's horn sounds a long blast may they approach the mountain." Exodus 19:9-13 (NIV)

Conditions of Covenant During the element of The Conditions of Covenant through this Blood Covenant Ceremony, we see how God begins His Conditions by stating how He has already shown His interest in and dedication to the Hebrew Children and will continue to do so if they will *"obey me fully and keep my covenant."* God continues to list for them all that He will do for them as His Conditions of Covenant and we see here just as The Blood Covenant Ceremony has within it, the other family deciding and then committing to the Conditions.

*"'You yourselves have seen what I did to Egypt, and how I carried you on eagles' wings and brought you to myself. 5 Now if you obey me fully and keep my covenant, then out of all nations you will be my treasured possession. Although the whole earth is mine, 6 you will be for me a kingdom of priests and a holy nation.' These are the words you are to speak to the Israelites."... **8 The people all responded together, "We will do everything the LORD has said." So Moses brought their answer back to the LORD."** Exodus 19:4-6,8 (NIV)*

The Conditions Continue. . .

"And God spoke all these words: 2 "I am the LORD your God, who brought you out of Egypt, out of the land of slavery. 3 "You shall have no other gods before me. 4 "You shall not make for yourself an idol in the form of anything in heaven above or on the earth beneath or in the waters below. 5 You shall not bow down to them or worship them; for I, the LORD your God, am a jealous God, punishing the children for the sin of the fathers to the third and fourth generation of those who hate me, 6 but showing love to a thousand generations of those who love me and keep my commandments.

7 "You shall not misuse the name of the LORD your God, for the LORD will not hold anyone guiltless who misuses his name. 8 "Remember the Sabbath day by keeping it holy. 9 Six days you shall labor and do all your work, 10 but the seventh day is a Sabbath to the LORD your God. On it you shall not do any work, neither you, nor your son or daughter, nor your manservant or maidservant, nor your animals, nor the alien within your gates. 11 For in six days the LORD made the heavens and the earth, the sea, and all that is in them, but he rested on the seventh day. Therefore the LORD blessed the Sabbath day and made it holy.

12 "Honor your father and your mother, so that you may live long in the land the LORD your God is giving you. 13 "You shall not murder. 14 "You shall not commit adultery. 15 "You shall not steal. 16 "You shall not give false testimony against your neighbor. 17 "You shall not covet your neighbor's house. You shall not covet your neighbor's wife, or his manservant or maidservant, his ox or donkey, or anything that belongs to your neighbor." Exodus 20:1-17 (NIV)

"Do not make any gods to be alongside me; do not make for yourselves gods of silver or gods of gold. 24 "'Make an altar of earth for me and sacrifice on it your burnt offerings and fellowship offerings, your sheep and goats and your cattle. Wherever I cause my name to be honored, I will come to you and bless you. 25 If you make an altar of stones for me, do not build it with dressed stones, for you will defile it if you use a tool on it. 26 And do not go up to my altar on steps, lest your nakedness be exposed on it.'" Exodus 20:23-26 (NIV)

Now there is SO MUCH MORE that Father God stated He would do in His part of The Conditions of The Covenant, and they can be found in their entirety in Chapters 21, 22 and 23 of Exodus. And when the people of Israel (One Covenant Family) were told by Moses ALL OF THESE CONDITIONS OF COVENANT that the other Covenant Family (Father God) said, they (Israel) responded:

*"When Moses went and told the people all the LORD's words and laws, **they responded with one voice, "Everything the LORD has said we will do." 4 Moses then wrote down everything the LORD had said. . ."** Exodus 24:3-4 (NIV))*

Now that both Covenant Families (Father God and Israel) spoke out of their mouths in agreement with each other about the terms of The Covenant they would have together, the two shall now move forward in the Covenant Ceremony state.

Representative Is Chosen Of course we can see throughout all of The Book of Exodus who was The Chosen Representative for Israel, that being Moses. And Father God was His own Family's (The Family of God) Representative. *Isn't it something that Father God was The Family of God's Covenant Representative in this Blood Covenant Ceremony, and His First Born, Jesus was The Family of God's Covenant Representative in The New Covenant that was cut!* The scriptures that clearly show us that Moses was The Chosen Representative for Israel are:

"Then Moses went up to God, and the LORD called to him from the mountain and said, "This is what you are to say to the house of Jacob and what you are to tell the people of Israel:" Exodus 19:3 (NIV)

"So Moses went back and summoned the elders of the people and set before them all the words the LORD had commanded him to speak." Exodus 19:7 (NIV)

Now we see in Exodus 19:18-25 that God Himself is The One representing His Family as The Covenant Representative. We see Him coming to the Covenant Site and meeting with the other family's Covenant Representative, Moses. When Father God, Who is representing His Family, descends on The Covenant Site, great signs of His arrival were displayed. The Bible says that fire, smoke, the trembling of the mountain and a trumpet sound all occurred. *(Remember, God came in the form of a smoking pot and a blazing torch (fire) when He came to The Blood Covenant Ceremony with Abraham. (Genesis 15:17-18) And now with Abraham's extended family, He shows up this way again, in smoke and fire!)*

Moses is called by God to come up to Him again and then directions are given to Moses, The Covenant Representative of The Hebrew People, on how The Other Covenant Representative, Father God, shall meet with Him. Father God tells Moses that no one shall come up the mountain, not even the priests, and details what will happen if the people try to. And then something very interesting happens. Father God tells Moses that one other may come up next time on the mountain with Moses, and it's his brother, Aaron.

"Mount Sinai was covered with smoke, because the LORD descended on it in fire. The smoke billowed up from it like smoke from a furnace, the whole mountain trembled violently, 19 and the sound of the trumpet grew louder and louder. Then Moses spoke and the voice of God answered him. 20 The LORD descended to the top of Mount Sinai and called Moses to the top of the mountain. So Moses went up 21 and the LORD said to him, "Go down and warn the people so they do not force their way through to see the LORD and many of them perish.

22 Even the priests, who approach the LORD, must consecrate themselves, or the LORD will break out against them." 23 Moses said to the LORD, "The people cannot come up Mount Sinai, because you yourself warned us, 'Put limits around the mountain and set it apart as holy.' " 24 The LORD replied, "Go down and bring Aaron up with you. But the priests and the people must not force their way through to come up to the LORD, or he will break out against them." 25 So Moses went down to the people and told them."
Exodus 19:18-25 (NIV)

What is awesome about this Pre-Covenant Cutting Meeting is that not only is Father God meeting with Moses, the other Covenant Representative, He is specifically telling Moses His Conditions prior to the Covenant Ceremony and as we said earlier, Father God is demonstrating Himself to

Moses and The Hebrew People in a similar manner as He did with Abraham, who was the one that the Covenant began with many years before them. Let's look at that again in verse 18 of Exodus 19 (NIV), which reads:

"Mount Sinai was covered with smoke, because the LORD descended on it in fire. The smoke billowed up from it like smoke from a furnace. . ."

And when we look at how God showed Himself to Abraham in that first Covenant Ceremony, we find in Genesis 15:17 (KJV) the same likeness:

"And it came to pass, that, when the sun went down, and it was dark, behold a smoking furnace, and a burning lamp that passed between those pieces."

Father God began His Covenant with Abraham and then He continued and added to the benefits with Moses and The Hebrew People and He did it by revealing Himself in the same manner! He was a smoking furnace and a burning lamp as fire in BOTH Blood Covenant Ceremonies!

In the first Blood Covenant Ceremony with Abraham only one man witnessed His form of the smoking furnace and the fire as a burning lamp. Yet later with Moses and the Hebrew People, they all could see glimpses of the smoke and burning of God on that mountain! What God began with Abraham in His Blood Covenant Ceremony, He continued with Moses and the Hebrew People! Even within the Covenant Ceremony Father God had with Abraham, we see God telling Abraham about his descendants that would come after him.

"Then the LORD said to him, "Know for certain <u>that your descendants will be strangers in a country not their own</u>, and <u>they will be enslaved and mistreated four hundred years</u>. 14 But I will punish the nation they serve as slaves, and afterward they will come out with

great possessions. 15 You, however, will go to your fathers in peace and be buried at a good old age." Genesis 15:13-15 NIV)

These people that would be enslaved and mistreated were the people Moses was now leading! And this extended family of Abraham was now seeing God in a mighty way! And as we said, when Abraham's family left Egypt they plundered the Egyptians and came out of that land with great possessions, just like God prophesied they would!

"And I will cause the Egyptians to look favorably on you. They will give you gifts when you go so you will not leave empty-handed. 22 Every Israelite woman will ask for articles of silver and gold and fine clothing from her Egyptian neighbors and from the foreign women in their houses. You will dress your sons and daughters with these, stripping the Egyptians of their wealth." Exodus 3:21-22 (NLT)

In addition, The Word says in verse 14, "but I will punish the nation they serve as slaves!" WOW! God was divinely predicting that Abraham's descendants would be slaves and they were! And I think plagues of darkness, flies, frogs and all the others could definitely be seen as to "punish" that Nation keeping Abraham's family enslaved, wouldn't you? God was prophesying at Abraham's Covenant Ceremony about the People He would continue and add further promises to, in the next Covenant Ceremony, which were Abraham's descendants, led by Moses! Both of these Ceremonies with Abraham and the Hebrew Children were tied together in how God's appearance was at both of them and the People the Covenants would be for–Abraham and his descendants! Let's look at the parallels in the Covenant Ceremonies. No wonder God showed Himself in similar manners at the Blood Covenant Ceremonies. . . **the first Covenant was a continuation of the other!**

Covenant Day On this very special day, all the families are to be present for the Blood Covenant Ceremony. All are to witness the Covenant Ceremony so that they will be able to tell their children, who shall tell their children and so on for the generations to come. WHO they are in Covenant with and WHAT are the Covenant Conditions they are entitled to is vital to know, for this crucial day would be passed on forever.

All of the Hebrew Children had come to the Covenant Ceremony prepared to come into this Holy Union with Father God. For we see in Exodus 19:14-15 that the People were consecrated; they washed themselves and set themselves apart for the Covenant Marriage Ceremony they were about to come into.

The families of the Hebrew Children face the other Family, Father God's, to which they are about to become in Covenant with by facing Mt. Sinai, which Father God is inhabiting. We see this very clearly taking place in the beginning stages of the Covenant Ceremony.

"Then Moses brought the people from the camp to meet God, and they stood at the foot of the mountain. 18 Mount Sinai was wrapped in smoke, for the Lord descended upon it in fire; its smoke ascended like that of a furnace, and the whole mountain quaked greatly."
Exodus 19:17-18 (AMP)

Both families (Israel and Father God) about to enter into Covenant are now facing each other. Israel is facing the mountain and Father God is facing them on the mountain.

Distant Shores Media/Sweet Publishing

We find in Chapters 20-23 of Exodus that Father God con- tinues to tell Moses all that He is expecting from The Hebrew People as they carry out their responsibilities of The Blood Covenant. The Ten Commandments, Laws on Idols and Building of Altars, Laws on how to treat people, Laws of Justice and Laws of Protection of Property, Social Responsibility, Laws of The Sabbath and the Annual Festivals and Feasts for the People were just some of the responsibilities that the Hebrew People had within their Covenant with God. And when Moses returned to the People to report all of these terms from Father God, we find the binding verbal agreement from the People to God's Covenant Conditions:

"When Moses went and told the people all the LORD's words and laws, they responded with one voice, "Everything the LORD has said we will do." 4 Moses then wrote down everything the LORD had said.. . ."
Exodus 24:3-4(NIV)

Both sides of the families coming into Covenant (Father God and the Hebrew People) have now stated their Covenant Conditions and have accepted them. The Conditions have been spoken and Moses then wrote all of the Covenant Conditions and acceptances proclaimed by both Covenant families.

Animal is Cut As always in a Blood Covenant Ceremony, there has to be blood. And we see that many animals were Cut for the Covenant Ceremony between The Hebrew Children and Father God. Again, during this Covenant, the families representing both sides of the families coming together in Covenant must be present. We find the detailed account in Exodus 24:4-8 (NIV) of how the sacrifice of the animals took place and the experiences of the People present for it.

". . . He got up early the next morning and built an altar at the foot of the mountain and set up twelve stone

pillars representing the twelve tribes of Israel. 5 Then he sent young Israelite men, and they offered burnt offerings and sacrificed young bulls as fellowship offerings to the LORD. 6 Moses took half of the blood and put it in bowls, and the other half he sprinkled on the altar.

7 Then he took the Book of the Covenant and read it to the people. They responded, "We will do everything the LORD has said; we will obey." 8 Moses then took the blood, sprinkled it on the people and said, "This is the blood of the covenant that the LORD has made with you in accordance with all these words."

Now, as we have written in detail throughout this Book, one of the things that is within a Blood Covenant Ceremony is that The Covenant Animal or Animals that have been selected **are brought to the center of the two families where the representatives are standing.** The Covenant Animals were put between Israel and Mt. Sinai where God was and were sacrificed. They are the best of the families' possessions. Father God is present on the top of Mt. Sinai, and at the bottom of the Mountain between God and the people, Moses builds an altar along with twelve stone pillars. So the animals being cut are placed in the center of the two families coming into Covenant.

After all the bulls from all the families are cut, Moses takes half the blood to pour on the altar and then takes the other half of the blood from the bulls and puts it in bowls. Moses once again reads the Covenant Conditions to the People that he had actually written down for them in a Book, so The Promises Are Proclaimed again for The Blood Covenant Ceremony, which is one of the steps. And once again, the Hebrew People speak that they will do everything the Lord has said and declare that they will obey.

Walk of Blood Then, as stated before, we read that Moses takes the remaining blood from the Covenant Animal and sprinkles it on the Covenant Family of People coming in Covenant with God.

> *"Moses then **took the blood, sprinkled it on the people** and said, "This is the blood of the covenant that the LORD has made with you in accordance with all these words."* Exodus 24:8 (NIV)

Because many families and tribes were a part of the Ceremony, the people would have blood **on them** as Representatives for the Hebrews. They had it on their bodies. So the Blood of the Covenant was placed on them and they "walked with the blood on them." Therefore fulfilling that, the Covenant Representatives would be standing with blood on them and even walking with the Covenant Blood on them, making several of them have a **"Walk of Blood"** during the Covenant Ceremony!

What an amazing continuation and addition to the Covenant that was Cut with Father Abraham and then onto Moses and the Hebrew People, Abraham's family. The Blood Covenant Ceremony sealed those promises and they are still blessing us today, as we are the seeds of Abraham!

> *"And now that you belong to Christ, you are the true children of Abraham. You are his heirs, and God's promise to Abraham belongs to you."* Galatians 3:29 (NLT)

Distant Shores Media/Sweet Publishing

Chapter Seven

BETWEEN TWO KINGS

". . . because he loved him as his own life. . ."
1 Samuel 18:3 (AMP)

I had read over the many Covenant Ceremonies for years as I would read The Word of God, not knowing what I was really looking at. Let us glance at one Covenant that was cut that would not only change two families but a Nation and a Kingdom. Let's go back into some history to truly see what transpired before this history-making Blood Covenant happened.

Israel was under the leadership of the Prophet Samuel. The people then decided that they did not want who God wanted to be their Leader, they wanted another. And the people did not want a man of God to lead them, they wanted a king.

"But when they said, "Give us a king to lead us," this displeased Samuel; so he prayed to the LORD. 7 And the LORD told him: "Listen to all that the people are saying to you; it is not you they have rejected, but they have rejected me as their king.. . . 9 Now listen to them; but warn them solemnly and let them know what the king who will reign over them will do.". . . 19 But the people refused to listen to Samuel. "No!" they said. "We want a king over us. . .". . . 21 When Samuel heard all that

*the people said, he repeated it before the LORD. 22 The
LORD answered, "Listen to them and give them a king."*
1 Samuel 8:6-7,9,19,21-22 (NIV)

So King Saul got the job of ruling Israel. Samuel continued
to be involved in King Saul's life and ministered to him regularly.

Then one day we find King Saul involved in a battle. He is
told specific directions from the Prophet Samuel and does not
obey and The Lord tells him that day through Samuel:

*"What have you done?" asked Samuel. 13 "You acted
foolishly," Samuel said. "You have not kept the command
the LORD your God gave you;* **if you had, he would
have established your kingdom over Israel for all
time.** *14 But now your kingdom will not endure; the LORD
has sought out a man after his own heart and appointed
him leader of his people, because you have not kept the
LORD's command." 1 Samuel 13:11,13-14 (NIV)*

And then we see King Saul's disobedience again in 1
Samuel 15. God told King Saul through the Prophet Samuel
to destroy all of the wicked Amalekites and all they possessed.
All their cattle, sheep, camels and donkeys - everything was
to be destroyed. But King Saul decides to spare Agag, their
King, and some of their choice animals. So God tells the
Prophet Samuel He is grieved that He made Saul King and
sends Samuel to him. At first, King Saul insists that he did
obey and only left the best of the animals to sacrifice to God
and then he is told, "To obey is better than sacrifice, and to
heed is better than the fat of rams" (Verse 22). Then God
speaks once more to King Saul through the Prophet Samuel,
another critical message.

*"But Samuel said to him, "I will not go back with you.
You have rejected the word of the LORD, and the LORD
has rejected you as king over Israel!" 27 As Samuel
turned to leave, Saul caught hold of the hem of his*

robe, and it tore. 28 Samuel said to him, "The LORD has torn the kingdom of Israel from you today and has given it to one of your neighbors—to one better than you. 29 He who is the Glory of Israel does not lie or change his mind; for he is not a man, that he should change his mind." 1Samuel 15:26-29 (NIV)

Then we find that the Prophet Samuel goes and finds Jesse and his son David in 1 Samuel 16, with a great purpose to complete. And what was Samuel and God's purpose? To anoint with oil a young man who had a heart like God to be the King of Israel.

The Positioning

The Bible tells us that the Spirit of The Lord leaves Saul and he begins to be tormented by an evil spirit. An attendant of his suggests that they find someone who can play the harp and relieve King Saul from the evil spirit. One knew of a son of Jesse that played and spoke very highly of David. King Saul sent for David and when he played for the King, the evil spirit would leave him.

The Bible also tells us that King Saul grew very fond of David and young David became his Armor Bearer (1 Samuel 16:14-23). Armor Bearers were known to always be committed to the one they were walking with and protecting and would give their lives for them. In battle they would hold the armor or shield in front of or behind the one they were protecting to guard them from weapons, arrows or attacks from the enemy. Their loyalty was constant and never-ending and they would be with that one, guarding him till death. God immediately began to position David in his inevitable destiny—toward the Kingship! And he began him by serving King Saul.

Then in Chapter 17 of First Samuel we see David being positioned again by God. Goliath, a Philistine from Gath, and his army were against Israel. As we all know, Goliath was huge and all of the Israelite army was afraid of him. David brings his brothers something to eat as they are with King Saul at the battle ground. It is known to others and told to David that whoever kills Goliath will receive from King Saul great wealth, the King's daughter in marriage and the victor and his family would also be granted exemption from taxes.

David finds himself in front of Saul and says he will go and fight Goliath. It's funny, King Saul makes David his Armor Bearer and he's in battle and has not asked David to be there with him. King Saul puts *his armor on his Armor Bearer, David.* Yet, it is too heavy and David takes it off. David says something very important about Goliath for what we will be seeing unveiled later. He says, *"Who is this uncircumcised Philistine that he should defy the armies of the living God?"* 1 Samuel 17:26 (NIV)

David was saying, *this man, Goliath has no Blood Covenant with God, Israel. Why are you afraid of him?* The word "uncircumcised" means that Goliath had no Blood Covenant with God. The Israelites were to be circumcised and that was their "mark" or Covenant Cut on their bodies that showed they were in Covenant with God. So David already knew that being in a Covenant with God would assure his victory, for God would be fighting for and with him! David declared his victory out loud (1 Samuel 17:45-47) and David killed Goliath of Gath and cut off his head.

> *"The king said, "Find out whose son this young man is." 57 As soon as David returned from killing the Philistine, Abner took him and brought him before Saul, with David still holding the Philistine's head. 58 "Whose son are you, young man?" Saul asked him. David said, "I am the son of your servant Jesse of Bethlehem."* 1 Samuel 17:56-58 (NIV)

As King Saul's Armor Bearer, David took his position seriously. He committed in his heart pure devotion to King Saul. And yet we see in 1 Samuel 17:55-58 Saul asking the commander of his army who David is! The respect and admiration that David had for King Saul was not returned to David, as we see very vividly in years to come. How sad. David always understood what it meant to be a servant and to have allegiance for another; King Saul never did.

When Everything Changed

The King, his army and David all returned to Israel and the women came out to greet them singing, *"Saul has slain his thousands, and David his tens of thousands"* 1Samuel 18:7 (NIV). And this made King Saul very angry and he had great jealousy for David. Now, part of the price for killing Goliath was the King's daughter. His firstborn was named Merab and yet she was given to another. But King Saul had another daughter Michal, who was used as a pawn on behalf of her own father. For we see in 1 Samuel 18:21,25 (NIV) Saul's thoughts and actions.

> *"I will give her to him," he thought, "so that she may be a snare to him and so that the hand of the Philistines may be against him." So Saul said to David, "Now you have a second opportunity to become my son-in-law.". .. 25 "Saul replied, "Say to David, 'The king wants no other price for the bride than a hundred Philistine foreskins, to take revenge on his enemies." Saul's plan was to have David fall by the hands of the Philistines."*

Michal was used only to snare David, and this deception was performed by her own father. And David had already given the price for the King's daughter in killing Goliath, but we see this was just a way that King Saul wanted David killed through the Philistines.

David paid again for the King's daughter with not just 100 lives and foreskins of the Philistines, but 200! Isn't it something that King Saul wanted the removal of the Philistines' foreskins which was the "mark," the circumcision of Covenant on the Israelites, but he wanted them from his enemies? King Saul never really appreciated or respected Blood Covenant, he never understood commitment or loyalty for others or the commitment and loyalty others had for him.

Knitted Together

The Bible tells us about two men destined for greatness - David, son of Jesse, and Jonathan, son of Saul. Their friendship went very deep; The Word of God says that in 1 Samuel:

"As soon as David returned from killing the Philistine, Abner took him and brought him before Saul, <u>with David still holding the Philistine's head</u>. 58 "Whose son are you, young man?" Saul asked him. David said, "I am the son of your servant Jesse of Bethlehem." (1Samuel 17:57-58 (NIV)).... "When David had finished speaking to Saul, the soul of Jonathan was knit with the soul of David, and Jonathan loved him as his own life. 2 Saul took David that day and would not let him return to his father's house." 1 Samuel 18:1-2 (AMP)

What differences there are in verses one and two of Chapter 18! The son of the King of Israel loved David and the father and King of Israel resented him. David's life had changed. He had killed Israel's enemy, Goliath, the Philistine. No one in Israel but David had the courage or faith to take down this enemy, not even Saul, the King himself. David stood before King Saul with Goliath's head in his hands and suddenly this young lad had all of Israel's attention. David had completed Saul's mission and now David was receiving all of King Saul's glory. King Saul would not allow David to return to his home or family after that day. He wanted to keep the person he saw as his enemy close to him.

But something else was going on in the room that day, as David stood there with the head of Goliath, Israel's enemy, in his hand before King Saul and Jonathan. A meeting of destiny between three Kings was occurring.

Saul, the present King of Israel, Jonathan, his son and future King of Israel and David, who had been told by God through the Prophet Samuel that he truly <u>would</u> <u>be</u> the King of Israel (1 Samuel 16:1-13), were all present, with all lives changing right there in that room together. Jonathan, the son of King Saul, would be getting a new "brother" and best friend. And David would be getting a new enemy in King Saul, Jonathan's father.

Making Destiny

David would now move into Jonathan's house and a Covenant Relationship would shortly begin.

*"Then Jonathan made **a covenant** with David, <u>because</u> <u>he loved him as his own life</u>. And Jonathan stripped himself of the robe that was on him and gave it to David, and his armor, even his sword, his bow, and his girdle."* 1 Samuel 18:3-4 (AMP)

Because the Word of God says, "Jonathan made a *covenant* with David," we know that a Blood Covenant Ceremony took place between these two young men. We are reminded that the word *covenant* is beriyth *(ber-eeth'),* which means **a compact made by passing between pieces of flesh.** We therefore know that a Covenant Animal was selected and the two Covenant Representatives for this Covenant Ceremony were Jonathan and David. The Covenant Animal would have been cut into two pieces and the halves placed facing each other while the blood drained out of both halves in the center to make that *"walkway of blood"* or *"alleyway* *of blood"* for the Representatives, David and Jonathan, to eventually stand in.

The Word tells us next that Jonathan took off his robe and gave it to David. Remember, the *Giving of the Coat or Robe* element of the Covenant Ceremony signifies that Jonathan was giving David <u>his</u> <u>authority</u>. *(Remember, when one Representative in The Blood Covenant Ceremony gives his robe to the other Representative, he is saying that all of his authority is now given to that other family!)*

In verse 4 of 1 Samuel 18, where we read about *the Giving of the Robe* between Jonathan and David, we find that the Hebrew word "robe" there is OT:4598 *me'iyl (meh-eel')* which means *in the sense of covering; a robe (i.e., upper and outer garment): a cloak, coat,* **mantle,** *robe.* Can we truly understand what was taking place here? Jonathan was King Saul's son and was next in line to be the King of Israel. Saul had been chosen by God, yet Saul did not obey God. And Jonathan was passing *his mantle and authority* over to David!

Due to King Saul's disobedience, God had made His decision to give the Kingship over to David. The very bloodline of King Saul, Jonathan, was coming into agreement with what God prophesied to David in that he would be Israel's next King! And the bloodline of the throne through Jonathan was now given to David by Covenant through the blood and by the Giving of the Coat or Robe, which is part of the Blood Covenant Ceremony! This Robe or Mantle of authority being passed from Jonathan (the next King to be of Israel) to David would change history forever for Israel and would pave the way for Jesus, Our King's bloodline, to come from King David! (Matthew 1:1-16) Amazing!

Distant Shores Media/Sweet Publishing

All My Strength

Next within the Blood Covenant Ceremony between Jonathan and David, The Word tells us that Jonathan gave David *"his armor, even his sword, his bow, and his girdle."* We know that within the Blood Covenant Ceremony there is the part within it that is called *The Trading of the Belts.* When Jonathan during this Covenant gave David his armor, sword, bow. . . all his weaponry and gave David his girdle or belt, Jonathan was conveying that David now had all of <u>his</u> <u>strength</u> and <u>support</u>.

Jonathan was coming into Covenant and establishing that David's enemies were now his enemies and that he would fight for David and with him. When one would go to battle, the other would go and fight with and for the other. How Jonathan loved his new brother and friend, David! King Saul saw David as his enemy and wanted to kill him and even tried several times (see 1 Samuel 18: 9-12). Because of this Blood Covenant Ceremony between Jonathan and David, Jonathan would later see that the biggest enemy that David would have would be his own father, King Saul. And because of this Covenant that Jonathan was now in with David, his father, King Saul would be his enemy, too.

Could Jonathan already see his father's jealousy that he had against David? I am sure that he could! His father would not even let David go home from the very beginning to his own father due to him killing Goliath! (1 Samuel 18:2) The women were singing songs about David killing ten thousands and Saul killing only in thousands after the killing of Goliath and that is when Saul began his overwhelming journey of resentment for David. The Bible tells us some very significant facts that Saul permits to happen in his life. And what Saul would speak in this time of evilness that he allowed would begin his destruction.

"This made Saul very angry. "What's this?" he said.
"They credit David with ten thousands and me with only

thousands. <u>Next they'll be making him their king!</u>" 9 So from that time on <u>Saul kept a jealous eye on David</u>.

10 The very next day a tormenting spirit from God overwhelmed Saul, <u>and he began to rave in his house like a madman</u>. David was playing the harp, as he did each day. But Saul had a spear in his hand, 11 and he suddenly hurled it at David, intending to pin him to the wall. But David escaped him twice. 12 Saul was then <u>afraid</u> of David, for the LORD was with David and had turned away from Saul." 1 Samuel 18:8-12 (NLT)

Jonathan would see on a daily basis his father acting in a manner of fear, jealousy, paranoia, like "a madman." Jonathan would know in his heart that choosing to come into a lifelong and life and death Blood Covenant would cost him every-thing. . . including his father!

I Give You My All

Later, after David has to eventually flee from King Saul and his home and hide in the wilderness, we find that Jonathan goes out to meet David and they make an addi-tional Covenant with each other.

*"David remained in the wilderness strongholds in the hill country of the Wilderness of Ziph. Saul sought him every day, but God did not give him into his hands. David saw that Saul had come out to seek his life. David was in the Wilderness of Ziph in the wood [at Horesh]. And Jonathan, Saul's son, rose and went into the wood to David [at Horesh] and strengthened his hand in God. He said to him, Fear not; the hand of Saul my father shall not find you. <u>You shall be king over Israel, and I shall be next to you. Saul my father knows that too</u>. And the two of them made **<u>a covenant</u>** before the*

Lord. And David remained in the wood [at Horesh], and Jonathan went to his house." 1 Samuel 23:14-18 (AMP)

Jonathan and David Cut another Blood Covenant. The Covenant Conditions were stated during the Covenant Ceremony. Jonathan very clearly expresses that his father, King Saul, is David's enemy and that David would be the new King of Israel, and that Jonathan would be beside him. Jonathan gave David his Robe and his armor, sword, bow and girdle in the first Blood Covenant Ceremony, therefore giving David his Authority and Strength. What Jonathan handed over to David that day during the Cutting of The Covenant was now manifesting through Jonathan's own understanding and words.

By this time, as Jonathan and David meet in the Wilderness of Ziph, Jonathan identifies that the Mantle or Robe of his and King Saul's Kingship over Israel was now David's and he is acknowledging it. Jonathan is stating at this Blood Covenant Ceremony with David that, *"You shall be king over Israel, and I shall be next to you. Saul my father knows that, too. And the two of them made **a covenant** before the Lord."* Jonathan began stating the *Conditions of the Covenant,* which is one of the elements of The Blood Covenant Ceremony, and at that very moment, Jonathan states that David shall be King of Israel!

Jonathan knew without a doubt what he was doing when he was Cutting The Blood Covenant with David! Jonathan knew that this wasn't some silly, childish gesture to be just a good friend to David. **No, Jonathan <u>knew</u> that he was giving his claim to being The Next King of Israel to David!** *(Let us not forget "covenant" means* beriyth *(ber-eeth'), which means **a compact made by passing between pieces of flesh.)*** And 1 Samuel 23:18 tells us that Jonathan and David made a "covenant" before The Lord. So we know that a Blood Covenant Ceremony happened between Jonathan and David that day in the desert. And when Jonathan states those Covenant Conditions during The Blood Covenant Ceremony that David *"shall be king over Israel,"* he "officially" and "legally" enables David to claim what had been prophesied and promised to David, and that was that David would be the King of Israel. Therefore, fulfilling yet another part of The Blood Covenant, which is **Combining the Covenant Families Names** – now David's name would combine with Jonathan's and King Saul's as *The King of Israel!*

The "Bloodline"

All Blood Covenant Ceremonies change history and yet again this one would change history forever, not just for two families, but also for a Nation and a Kingdom over which a King would sit that would last forever! The Covenant Animal is sliced in half and both men are standing face to face with each other and stating the *Conditions of Covenant* to each other while standing inside of the blood and entrails of that *Covenant Animal.* Only through *blood* could David "lawfully" be the King of Israel, and through *blood* he was. Jonathan merged David, through the Blood Covenant Ceremony, while standing in blood, into Jonathan's own family, therefore placing David in Jonathan's **"bloodline"** and able to be the King. This Covenant Ceremony would merge David into being a "blood" brother to Jonathan and a "blood" son to King Saul, who is the sitting King of Israel.

The Blood Covenant Ceremony merged their two families together. David was the *Covenant Representative* for his family and Jonathan was the *Covenant Representative* for his. Jonathan relinquished his Kingship that day and stated his and his father's, King Saul's places. He told David while standing in that Covenant Animal's Blood that <u>David</u> would be the King of Israel, therefore Jonathan would not be and King Saul would no longer be, and Jonathan stated that his father knew it. However, the day that we see that Jonathan died, he was with his father, King Saul, in battle instead of who he was truly in Covenant with, his brother and friend whom he loved, David. (1 Samuel 31:1-4)

When Jonathan gave David his robe, he legally made a way for the throne and Kingship of Israel to be given to ***David and his bloodline.*** For when two families come into Blood Covenant together, the families merge together! Remember the example of the Smith family and the Jones family cutting a Blood Covenant with each other? And even their names uniting? This happened through the Blood Covenant Ceremony and the Giving of the Coat or Robe (Jonathan's mantle of future King) between Jonathan and David and the Trading of the Belts (Jonathan's strength) segment of this Covenant Ceremony. God knew King Saul would not give up his throne, so God did it through the love of the King's son for another and through the Blood Covenant Ceremony. This is how David was "legally" able to be the next King of Israel. He had to become a part of King Saul's family and "bloodline." And the transaction happened at the Blood Covenant Ceremony between Jonathan and David.

Only through *blood* can a person or persons be fused into another's family. And for David to be the King of Israel, he had to be joined with King Saul's (the King of Israel's) family by "blood." And for David to be the King of Israel, he had to be a "blood" son of King Saul. For it is protocol for one to become the King to be a son and heir to the King. One can only have the Kingship by being **an heir.** And the only way to lawfully be an heir is through **blood relation.** God knew that King Saul would NOT hand over his dominion and authority, so God decides to use Saul's son.

God allows the unselfishness of a son to a very selfish and prideful King to have the son's heart be knitted to David. And while that hard and selfish King wasn't looking, the knitting of his own son's heart was taking place. King Saul's son placed himself in Covenant with the very one that God had chose to be King.

The only one on Earth who could legally give David this position was Jonathan! Yes, God had said that David was to be the King of Israel and that King Saul would not continue to be the King and prophetically that is what happened. Yet God follows protocol, too! Jonathan was the next to have the throne of Israel. So the one who had the right was the only one who could give it away! The next blood heir to Saul's throne had to legally give it to another, and it would only be legal through. . . BLOOD! The Blood Covenant Ceremony, to be exact!

David was not birthed into Saul's family or blood line. Yes, he was brought into a Marriage Covenant with King Saul's daughter Michal, but it was to *snare* David (1 Samuel 18:21). Only a *True Love from another* in Covenant with *a Pure Form of* Love could bring forth God's Plan in making David the Next King of Israel, not trickery. God had to use a member of King Saul's family to merge David into Covenant with King Saul, not as a "snare" but truly merging their very hearts. . . . And God could not use Michal, He could not use King Saul, so God used Jonathan.

For, God could only use someone from King Saul's, The King of Israel's, bloodline who understood and possessed real love. No manipulation, only pure love, selfless love, sacrificing love. . . as Jonathan had and did for David. Because God's Son Jesus would be in the bloodline of King David, the Blood Covenant that brought King David into the bloodline of The King of Israel HAD TO BE PURE AND SELFLESS, JUST LIKE JESUS WOULD BE! The Bloodline that grafted David into The King of Israel would also be used to bring forth Jesus, The King of Israel! The first King of Israel, Saul, had manipulated the Kingship. God needed someone *"like His own heart"* (1 Samuel 13:14) to correct what was wrong for Jesus to sit on that throne forever.

The beauty of Jonathan's heart amazes me. The sacrifice of giving your entitlement to hold the highest and most powerful throne in the World and to do it with all humility and sincerity to another–that's really beautiful. Yet, just that type of love was given to you and me through Jesus. Just like Jonathan did for David, Jesus made us to be His Family. He made us kings and priests (Revelation 5:10) and made us royalty! He gave us His strength and His authority.

The King of Israel's Position became pure again for Jesus through Jonathan, so that Jesus, The King of Israel, could legally sit on The King of Israel's Throne after it had been defiled by King Saul. One would have to exemplify true, pure love, for Love, which is God, Himself. . . and the one God used was The First King of Israel's son, a boy named Jonathan.

1 Samuel 18:1,3 *"When David had finished speaking to Saul, the soul of Jonathan was knit with the soul of David, and Jonathan loved him as his own life. . . . 3 Then Jonathan made a covenant with David, because he loved him as his own life."*

"No one has greater love [no one has shown stronger affection] **than to lay down (give up) his own life for his friends.***"* John 15:13 (AMP)

And that is exactly what Jonathan did. . . he loved David and gave *his reign, his future, his heir, his life for his friend.* As we will see Jesus would do for us, his friends, too! *Beautiful!*

Chapter Eight

A WALK TO REMEMBER

*"After the men who were carrying the
Ark of the Lᴏʀᴅ had gone six steps. . ."*
2 Samuel 6:13 (NLT)

*W*e have discussed that Israel's Kings did not always do what God had directed for them and the Nation to do. We've talked in detail about King David and how he became the King of Israel through The Blood Covenant he had with Jonathan, and yet there's such a significant event in his life that happened that we must talk about. King David, who was described by God as a man after His own heart (1 Samuel 13:14), was called to bring God's Presence back to His People. The weight of this one assignment was of enormous measure! **The Ark of The Covenant, which carried the Presence of God and The Promises made between God and His People at Mt. Sinai in it, had not been in The People of God's presence for nearly <u>100 years</u>!** King David would soon discover the weight of this mission of transporting The Ark and carrying God's Presence.

Copying. . . Your Enemies?

History tells us King David and others with him attempted to move The Ark, God's Presence, without knowing from God HOW to do so. The first time David and the Leaders of Israel began moving The Ark of The Covenant, it appears that he might have followed some of the blueprints of the Philistines when they moved The Ark.

We find in 1 Samuel that the Philistines, Israel's enemy, had possession of The Ark of The Covenant and because they did, destruction began to come to them. Mice overtook the Philistines and very painful tumors or boils came on them due to them having The Ark of The Covenant in their midst. The "war trophy" they thought they had in possessing The Ark of The Covenant was not a "trophy" for them at all!

They sought the counsel of the leaders of the Philistines on how to get rid of The Ark of The Covenant and finally they came up with the plan to put The Ark on a new cart they made with two cows yoked together to pull the new cart. They had no one to lead this cart; they let the animals pulling it just take it away!

The cart with The Ark of The Covenant finally arrived at Kiriath-jearim. It should be noted that the land of Kiriath-jearim belonged to the Tribe of Judah. (*Remember, Jesus is The Lion of The Tribe of Judah!*) And the cart with the two cows pulling it and The Ark of The Covenant on the cart arrived at a man's house named Abinadab in Kiriath-jearim. Abinadab and his son, Eleazar became the ones in charge of The Ark of The Covenant. The Ark stayed there nearly <u>100 years</u>!

"And the ark remained in Kiriath-jearim a very long time [nearly 100 years, through Samuel's entire judgeship, Saul's reign, and well into David's, when it was brought to Jerusalem]. For it was twenty years before all the house of Israel lamented after the Lord." 1 Samuel 7:2 (AMP)

Mission: Not Accomplished

King David knew that he had an assignment from God, and that was to bring God's Presence to Jerusalem. David assembled the People of Israel that day to move The Ark of The Covenant and it wasn't just a few, it was **30,000 people to be exact!**

> ***"Again David gathered together all the chosen men of Israel, 30,000."*** 2 Samuel 6:1 (AMP)

David and 30,000 others were before The Lord (The Ark of The Covenant) and their plan was to move that Ark from Kiriath-jearim to Jerusalem. *"And David and all Israel went up to Baalah, that is, to Kiriath-jearim which belonged to Judah, to bring up from there the ark of God the Lord. . . "* 1 Chronicles 13:6 (AMP)

> *"And David and all the house of Israel played before the Lord with all their might, with songs, lyres, harps, tambourines, castanets, and cymbals."* 2 Samuel 6:5 (AMP)

The Bible says that all the people played instruments and praised God with all their might. See, David and the House of Israel were transporting The Ark of The Covenant with the right heart, *they just were doing it the wrong way!* For we see King David and the Leaders of Israel taking a very similar action to that of the Philistines.

> *"And they set the ark of God upon <u>a new cart</u> and brought it out of the house of Abinadab, which was on the hill; and Uzzah and Ahio, sons of Abinadab, drove the <u>new cart</u>. . . . And when they came to Nacon's threshing floor, Uzzah put out his hand to the ark of God and took hold of it, for <u>the oxen</u> stumbled and shook it."* 2 Samuel 6:3,6 (AMP)

Distant Shores Media/Sweet Publishing

King David and the Leaders of Israel made a "new cart" and put animals with it to pull it while The Ark of The Covenant was on it. This was NOT how God said to transport His Presence, The Ark. Yet, King David and the Leaders of Israel knew that the Philistines had moved The Ark 100 years ago with a new cart and some animals pulling it. So, instead of doing it the way God had said, they trusted what others did (and those "others" were their enemies, the Philistines.)

When that new cart stumbled with God's Presence on it and Uzzah touched it, he died. The Bible says that the oxen were moving The Ark of The Covenant and they stumbled at a place called a threshing floor. 1 Chronicles 13:9 (AMP) translates it, "to the threshing floor of Chidon." In 2 Samuel 6:6 (AMP) it translates that David and all of Israel came to "Nacon's threshing floor." Upon research of "Chidon" or "Nacon" it was found that it could mean a person's name that had a threshing floor or the place of that threshing floor, which means that the oxen may have noticed the grain at the threshing floor and that might have made a difference in their movement when the Ark shook. *"Nacon"* means *"firm"* or *"prepared."* And as we know, David and the Leaders of Israel were *not "prepared"* in their measures in moving the Ark of The Covenant.

> *"For because you bore it not [as God directed] at the first, the Lord our God broke forth upon us—because we did not seek Him in the way He ordained."* 1 Chronicles 15:13 (AMP)

King David and the people of Israel did not seek God, for if they had they would have found that the only way God ordained to move The Ark of The Covenant was for only the Levites to carry The Ark by poles. The King and people of Israel were *not prepared* for this important and history-changing transport and that is why Uzzah lost his life at this threshing floor, called *"Nacon."*

Right Heart, Wrong Way!

King David became grieved, offended, and the Bible says he was afraid of The Lord that day. And he thought that no one could do this assignment of transport (2 Samuel 6:8-10). He thought:

"We had a new cart, I and 30,000 people were all praising God and rejoicing and playing instruments in moving it and because a good man reached out and touched The Ark when it stumbled, he dies! How could anyone get this Ark to Jerusalem?"

So David, after Uzzah died while on that route to Jerusalem, decided to not go any further! Can you imagine? Over 30,000 people all together with one mission in mind and all rejoicing, for they were bringing to Jerusalem The Presence of God! And then because King David and the Leaders of Israel DID NOT TAKE THE TIME TO SEE HOW TO MOVE GOD, they cost a man his life and must have looked very lowly in the people's eyes that day. I would imagine that King David's leadership was questioned that day by many. So David, out of what The Bible says was offense and fear, sent The Ark of The Covenant to a MAN'S HOUSE, named Obed-edom.

"So David did not bring the ark home to the City of David, but carried it aside into the house of Obed-edom ***the Gittite*** *[a Levitical porter born in Gath-rimmon]."*
1 Chronicles 13:13 (AMP)

Isn't that something? King David decides in the middle of this parade with 30,000 people to just take The Ark of The Covenant to a man's house! David must have known that a Levite could handle The Ark. And so he took it to the nearest one on the route! If only David had used that knowledge of WHO was supposed to be handling The Ark in the first place! Again, King David and the House of Israel were transporting

The Ark of The Covenant with the right heart; *they just were doing it the wrong way!*

The Ark of The Lord stayed at Obed-edom's house for three (3) months. The Bible states that with The Ark being at his home, great blessings happened to his household (1 Chronicles 13:14). We also know that from Obed-Edom's house, The Ark would eventually go to The City of David, Jerusalem (1 Chronicles 15:29) and be placed in a tent King David prepared for it outside the Palace of David. (1 Chronicles 15:1).

King David, the Priests and the People of Israel were all moving before The Ark of God, transporting The Ark together that day on that new cart they had built before Uzzah died. They all had good intentions and wanted to obey God in getting The Ark of The Covenant to Jerusalem. And we have learned that The Ark was never to be transported on a cart, it was to be carried by the Levites.

Yet there was one more very important element missing in addition to not carrying The Ark of The Covenant correctly, and that missing element was – *Blood!* David would soon discover the accurate way to bring God back to His People, and he would find the answers within The Blood Covenant Ceremony. Let's look at The Blood Covenant Ceremony again.

Looking Back, So You Can Go Forward

As we have seen, the first attempt to move The Ark of The Covenant was A HUGE FAILURE. So let's look at some of the preparations that were made in the second attempt by King David and the people of Israel. And what was the key element in moving The Ark of The Covenant the second time? The answer is doing it God's Way, with The Blood Covenant Ceremony!

The Representatives for The Blood Covenant Ceremony were chosen. God was present in The Ark and He Himself was one of the Representatives in this Covenant Ceremony. All of the House of Israel, King David, the priests, the musicians and singers were gathered jointly, being all together the other Representatives in this Blood Covenant Ceremony.

Many of these same Representatives had been present for the first failed transport of The Ark of The Covenant when Uzzah died and at that attempt there were 30,000 people. To transport The Ark, King David and the People of God went back and found out the Ways of The Lord and it was through Blood Covenant that they found most of their answers. The Covenant Representatives of God Himself and King David and all the people of Israel were chosen and in place.

The Covenant Site was chosen, and it would be the roads and paths traveled by both parties of Representatives (The People of Israel with King David and God). It would be on these roads and paths that the second transport occurred from the house of Obed-edom to the City of David, and then unto the tent that was set in place and pitched for The Ark of God's Presence to remain (2 Samuel 6:10, 12, 17).

God and His People would travel on those roads to Jerusalem together through this Covenant Ceremony, then enter into the Walls of Jerusalem and then finally to the site of the tent that King David had erected for God in The Ark. This Covenant Ceremony Site for this Blood Covenant Ceremony that King David and the House of Israel were doing with God was not just one place and stationary; this Covenant Site was upon the roads from Obed-edom's house to Jerusalem and through the City of Jerusalem. This Covenant Site would be mobile, *very mobile.*

The Conditions of The Covenant were placed, of course, in part within The Ark of The Covenant–the tablets containing The Ten Commandments given to Moses. The very first Conditions of The Covenant were given to Abraham and then more Conditions of The Covenant were added on with Moses and the Hebrew Children at the bottom and on the top of Mt. Sinai.

And then we see in scriptures that Covenant Promises and Decrees were proclaimed by David, who Blessed and Declared them during The Blood Covenant Ceremony as he addressed The Lord and The People present that day (see 1

Chronicles 16:8-36). As David, the Covenant Representative, decreed Conditions and praises, the other fellow Israelites and Witnesses of the Covenant Ceremony that day responded to the Promises and Decrees proclaimed by David at this Blood Covenant Ceremony:

> *". . . Then all the people said "Amen"* (which means so be it) *and "Praise The Lord."* 1 Chronicles 16:36

All of the Family of King David and All The House of Israel came into agreement with each other and with God on this Covenant Day.

The Animal is Cut element of The Blood Covenant Ceremony, as we've talked about before, was normally with one or two animals. Let's recall the description and details that we have covered previously to remind us of this very important part of the Blood Covenant Ceremony. This will be very crucial in recapping to see what really happened in this second attempt to bring The Ark of The Covenant to Jerusalem.

One or two Animals are selected by the two parties or families that are coming together in Covenant. The Animal(s) are to be the best that the two families have to offer. The Animal(s) given to represent each family are sacrificed. The Covenant Cut is performed on each of these Animals.

This Cut is to slice the Covenant Animals right down the middle of their spines, making the two halves of the Animals to fall open, and each half opposite of each other. In the center of the two halves of the Animal(s) a natural blood flow occurs. Blood from within both sides of the Animal(s) that have been cut flows to the ground between the two halves of flesh. If more than two Animals are used, the Covenant Animals are placed *right in front of or behind the other Animals,* **making a walkway or alleyway of blood between the two halves of Animals!**

Walk of Blood After this, the two Covenant Representatives chosen from the two families or persons coming into Covenant make the Walk of Blood. As the

Covenant Animal(s) has been cut into two halves, the Representatives then walk between the two halves that have fallen apart and are opposite each other. The blood that has drained from the two halves of these Animals into the center by this time is very deep.

The Representatives for the families walk through the "blood alley." They are ankle to knee deep in blood. The smell, the feeling and sight of the raw flesh, organs, guts and blood all around their feet, ankles and legs are overwhelming! Possibly the undigested food that was in the animal, now laying out of it or in the blood that they now stand and walk in, is very difficult to bear. This is an experience that The Blood Covenant Representatives, nor the Covenant Families watching will NEVER FORGET! *(Taken from previous data written in this book, The Bride & The Blood Covenant Ceremony.)*

Chapter Nine

THE COLOR RED

". . . David and all the people of Israel. . ."
2 Samuel 6:15 (NLT)

*D*avid had thousands of people there that day on the second attempt to move The Ark of The Covenant! There were the men who had consecrated themselves, the Levites who were to carry The Ark, God's Presence in The Ark of The Covenant, King David, the singers and musicians and "ALL The House of Israel" (2 Samuel 6:15) were present and were before the Levites who were carrying The Ark of The Covenant (God)!

All the people present were praising, playing music, blowing the ram's horns, singing and dancing before God on this second Transport of The Ark! For we know it was even more imperative that this second Transport be completed, and King David and all the Israelites praised, danced, sang and worshiped during the first attempted transport of The Ark:

> *"And David and all the house of Israel played <u>before the Lord</u> with all their might, with songs, lyres, harps, tam-bourines, castanets, and cymbals."* 2 Samuel 6:5 (AMP)

And where was God, The Other Representative making Covenant, that day? His Presence and Promises were in

The Ark of The Covenant that was being carried! And in the second transport of The Ark, we see where the other Covenant Representatives coming into Covenant were:

"And David danced <u>before</u> the L<small>ORD</small> *with all his might, wearing a priestly garment. 15 <u>So David and all the</u> <u>people of Israel</u> brought up the Ark of the* L<small>ORD</small> *with shouts of joy and the blowing of rams' horns."* 2 Samuel 6:14-15 (NLT)

In this amazing and huge procession shouts, singing, sounds of musical instruments and ram's horns and dancing were all <u>ahead</u> of The Ark of The Covenant, all before God's Presence. King David, the musicians, the singers and all the People of Israel were preparing the way and preparing the atmosphere for God and His Presence! As God was carried in, He was carried in on Praise and Worship! Hallelujah! All of the People who were involved in this Blood Covenant Ceremony were present and participating, not just observing, this day!

Yet, as we begin to picture in our minds the "lineup" of <u>who</u> was present at this Blood Covenant Ceremony and how they were in motion and in a constant state of Praise and Worship, we cannot get a full picture in our minds of what this looked like, until we add the color **red.** We cannot conceive what the complete image of all of this looked like until we look at all of this marvelous motion of people and God - ***all in blood!***

"Now it was told King David, saying, "The L<small>ORD</small> *has blessed the house of Obed-Edom and all that belongs to him, because of the ark of God." So David went and brought up the ark of God from the house of Obed-Edom to the City of David with gladness. **13 And so it was, <u>when those bearing the ark of the Lord had gone six</u> <u>paces</u>, that he sacrificed <u>oxen</u> and <u>fatted sheep</u>.** 14 Then David **<u>danced before the Lord</u>** with all his might; and David was wearing a linen ephod. 15 So <u>David</u> and <u>all the house of Israel</u> brought up the ark of the* L<small>ORD</small>

*with shouting and with the sound of the trumpet.. . . So they brought the ark of the LORD, and set it in its place in the midst of the tabernacle that David had erected for it. **Then David offered burnt offerings and peace offerings before the LORD.**"* (2 Samuel 6:12-15, 17 New King James Version (NKJV)

(NOTE: The word "Oxen" is plural of "ox" meaning more than one.

In some translations of The Bible it states that one "ox" or "fatling" was sacrificed. And yet many other translations clearly reveal more than one. I believe that *at least one ox and one lamb were sacrificed, if not more than one each!* And as we look at this further, you will clearly see why!

Let's really pay attention here. We are talking about **a sacrifice of two animals <u>EVERY SIX STEPS</u> – an ox and a fatted lamb! And how we can know that it WAS every six paces is that The Bible tells us that it was "oxen" or "fatlings" or "fattened animals!" We are seeing in <u>many</u> Translations of The Word that the Animals are PLURAL! That means NOT JUST ONE OF THESE ANIMALS OF EACH KIND WAS USED! We are talking about sacrifices of MANY ANIMALS!**

Other translations that illustrate and confirm these amazing sacrifices are:

*"And it was so that, when those who bore the ark of the LORD had gone <u>six paces</u>, he sacrificed **oxen** and **fatlings**."* 2 Samuel 6:13, (21 Century King James Version) (KJ21)

*"After those who were carrying the ark of the LORD had taken six steps, he sacrificed **oxen** and **fattened animals,** dancing in front of the LORD with all of his strength and wearing a linen ephod."* 2 Samuel 6:13-14 (International Standard Version)

*". . .and brought up the Chest of God from the house of Obed-Edom to the City of David, celebrating extravagantly all the way, **with frequent sacrifices of choice bulls.**"* (The Message Bible)

Now that we have established that there were MANY animals that were sacrificed that day on the second Transport of The Ark of The Covenant, let's look at the distance the Covenant Families came. *This is going to amaze you!*

How Long Away?

Now, we know that King David and 30,000 people began the First Transport of The Ark of The Covenant from Kiriath-jearim to Jerusalem.

"And David and all Israel went up to Baalah, that is, to Kiriath-jearim, which belonged to Judah, to bring up from there the ark of God the Lord. . ." 1 Chronicles 13:6 (AMP)

And we have addressed that David and the House of Israel were transporting The Ark of The Covenant with the right heart, *they just were doing it the wrong way!* And that they were following the way the Philistines had moved The Ark, with a cart and cows pulling it. And we have established that when the cart being pulled by the oxen when King David was moving it went by a threshing floor at Nacon, the oxen stumbled and Uzzah touched it and died. David then fearfully takes The Ark to a man named Obed-edom's house. So we know that *this Second Transport begins at Obed-edom's house!*

Now let's do some math! We know the first attempt began at Kiriath-jearim. And as always, the destination that King David was moving The Ark to was Jerusalem. From Kiriath-jearim to Jerusalem is approximately 10 miles.

Now, many, many hours have been set aside to research EXACTLY where Obed-edom lived on the route from

Kiriath-jearim to Jerusalem. And to our regret it could not be found within The Word and even through ancient maps of Israel. The specific location of Obed-edom's house or the specific location of Nacon's threshing floor cannot be found. But we do know FOR SURE that it is approximately 10 miles from where the first Transport began at Kiriath-jearim to Jerusalem. SEE MAP.

Map 4: LAND OF THE TWELVE TRIBES

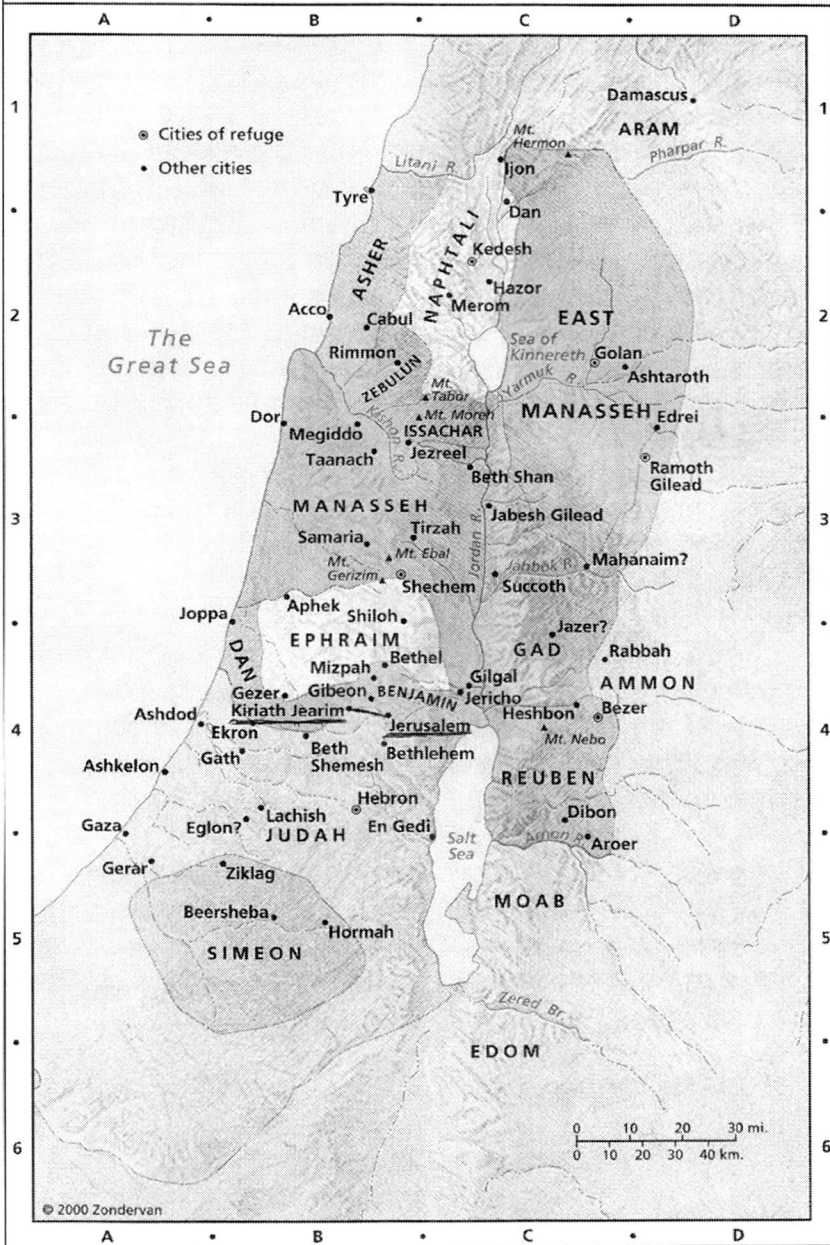

A • B • C • D

⊚ Cities of refuge
• Other cities

The
Great Sea

Damascus
ARAM
Mt. Hermon
Litani R.
Ijon
Pharpar R.
Tyre
Dan
ASHER
Kedesh
NAPHTALI
Hazor
Acco
Merom
Cabul
EAST
Rimmon
Sea of Kinnereth
Golan
ZEBULUN
Ashtaroth
Dor
Mt. Tabor
Mt. Moreh
Yarmuk R.
MANASSEH
Edrei
Megiddo
ISSACHAR
Taanach
Jezreel
Beth Shan
Ramoth Gilead
MANASSEH
Jabesh Gilead
Tirzah
Samaria
Jordan R.
Mt. Gerizim
Mt. Ebal
Jabbok R.
Mahanaim?
Shechem
Succoth
Joppa
Aphek
Shiloh
Jazer?
EPHRAIM
GAD
Rabbah
Mizpah
Bethel
AMMON
Gezer
Gibeon
BENJAMIN
Gilgal
Jericho
Bezer
Ashdod
Kiriath Jearim
Heshbon
Ekron
Jerusalem
Mt. Nebo
Ashkelon
Gath
Beth Shemesh
Bethlehem
REUBEN
Hebron
Gaza
Eglon?
Lachish
En Gedi
Dibon
JUDAH
Salt Sea
Arnon R.
Aroer
Gerar
Ziklag
MOAB
Beersheba
Hormah
SIMEON
Zered Br.
EDOM

0   10   20   30 mi.
0   10   20   30   40 km.

© 2000 Zondervan

A • B • C • D

So, to get a good picture of what actually happened and what it looked like when King David and all The House of Israel were doing the Second Transport of The Ark let's look at an example of the extreme endeavor that these followers of God undertook.

We know that from Kiriath-jearim to Jerusalem is approximately 10 miles. And we know that on the first Transport of The Ark that Kiriath-jearim is where they left from. So, just for an example, we <u>do</u> know that King David and the people of Israel did go some distance within that 10 mile journey, but then stopped due to Uzzah touching the Ark and dying. Therefore, let's again, just for an example, say that David and the people of Israel got 4 miles on their route to Jerusalem accomplished, leaving 6 more miles to go.

There are approximately 2,000 steps within a mile. And we are saying as an example that there is 6 miles to go. So, 2,000 steps multiplied by 6 would equal 12,000 steps. The Bible says that:

*". . . So David went and brought up the ark of God from the house of Obed-Edom to the City of David with gladness. **13 And so it was, <u>when those bearing the ark of the Lord had gone six paces</u>, that he sacrificed oxen and fatted sheep.**"* (2 Samuel 6:12-13 (NKJV))

For every six steps a sacrifice happened *of at least* 1 ox and 1 lamb. 12,000 steps divided by 6 steps (or paces) equals **2,000 stops to sacrifice.** And sacrificing an ox and a lamb at each stop, that would equal **2,000 oxen** and **2,000 sheep upon arriving in Jerusalem!** It would look like this:

**6 Miles To Jerusalem at 2,000 Steps Per Mile
= 12,000 Steps
12,000 Steps ÷ 6 Steps (or Paces)
= 2,000 Stops To Sacrifice
1 Ox and 1 Lamb Sacrificed At 2,000 Stops
= 2,000 Oxen and 2,000 Sheep**

And this would be the calculations for an example if there were 6 miles to go to bring The Ark to Jerusalem. *Now I know that seems absolutely over-the-top extreme! It's almost too much to even picture, isn't it?* But let's look at this incredible truth and we'll see so clearly together how serious and realistic this really is Church!

Like Father, Like Son

Another Truth that we know is that David's son Solomon moved The Ark of The Covenant from one place to another place inside of Jerusalem and The Bible says that there were SO MANY SACRIFICES OF ANIMALS in that move of The Ark *that you could not even count how many animals were sacrificed! And where do you think Solomon learned How To Move The Ark of The Covenant in Blood from? Of course, his father, King David!*

> *"King Solomon and all the congregation of Israel who had assembled before him WERE WITH HIM BEFORE THE ARK, SACRIFICING SHEEP AND OXEN, SO MANY THAT THEY COULD NOT BE REPORTED OR COUNTED."* **1 Kings 8:5 (AMP)**

The Bible is telling us here that Solomon and "all the congregation of Israel" is with him and they are all sacrificing animals before The Ark of The Covenant! And there are so many animals being sacrificed before The Ark *that they cannot be reported or counted!* The Covenant Cut is being administered to these Covenant Animals and thousands of people with Solomon and the Levites that are carrying The Ark are all walking through these countless Covenant Animals! All are making The Walk of Blood while they transport The Ark of The Covenant! Is this sounding familiar?

And we see in 1 Kings 8:5 that during the movement of The Ark, The Bible says so many animals were used that you could not count them. And yet, when we read on in 1 Kings we find ANOTHER SACRIFICE and OFFERING by Solomon! When he arrives at The Temple Site with The Ark, The Bible says that Solomon performs a Sacrifice of Fellowship Offering or what they also referred to as a Peace Offering.

"And the king, and all Israel with him, offered sacrifice before the LORD. 63 And Solomon offered a sacrifice of peace offerings, which he offered unto the LORD, two and twenty thousand oxen, and an hundred and twenty thousand sheep. So the king and all the children of Israel dedicated the house of the LORD."
1 Kings 8:62-63 (KJV)

Can we wrap our minds around those numbers? King Solomon and the People of Israel gave as an offering To The Lord **22,000 oxen** and **120,000 sheep!** Now, what is extremely important here is that *we know exactly how many animals they sacrificed when they arrived at the Temple Site (22,000 oxen and 120,000 sheep)! Yet in 1 Kings 8:5, The Word says so many oxen and sheep were sacrificed THAT THEY COULD NOT BE COUNTED!*

One scripture states that the sacrifices could not be counted, the other scripture gives us exact totals. That is because we are talking about two different instances! We have a specific amount of how many animals were sacrificed for God at the Temple when they arrived (22,000 oxen and 120,000 sheep.) BUT WHILE MOVING THE ARK OF THE COVENANT TO THE TEMPLE it was so many that it could not be counted or reported!

So, if Solomon had 142,000 oxen and sheep added together and sacrificed at The Temple when it was time to dedicate it, and so many Covenant Animals Cut that it could not be counted or recorded while moving and bringing The Ark of The Covenant to The Temple, **then why would we be astonished that King David would make a sacrifice of two Covenant Animals (an ox and a lamb) every six paces** while he moved The Ark from Obed-edom's house to Jerusalem? This IS HOW David discovered how to move The Ark of The Covenant–through The Blood Covenant Ceremony! *King David gave enormously in the 1,000s of Covenant Animals, why wouldn't his son, King Solomon?*

And to show even more that Solomon followed his father's way in moving The Ark, we see that The Word tells us that King Solomon sacrificed the same animals as King David did when he moved The Ark of The Covenant, and that was oxen and sheep.

> *"Now it was told King David, saying, "The LORD has blessed the house of Obed-Edom and all that belongs to him, because of the ark of God." So David went and brought up the ark of God from the house of Obed-Edom to the City of David with gladness.* **13 And so it was, <u>when those bearing the ark of the LORD had gone six paces,</u> that he sacrificed <u>OXEN</u> and <u>FATTED SHEEP.</u>** 2 Samuel 6:12-13 (NKJV)

> **"King Solomon and all the congregation of Israel who had assembled before him WERE WITH HIM <u>BEFORE THE ARK,</u> <u>SACRIFICING SHEEP AND OXEN,</u> <u>SO</u> <u>MANY</u> <u>THAT</u> <u>THEY</u> <u>COULD</u> <u>NOT</u> <u>BE REPORTED</u> OR <u>COUNTED.</u>"** 1 Kings 8:5 (AMP)

How Will I Know?

How did King Solomon know the Operational Procedures on "How To Move (God) The Ark of The Covenant?" **From the very Blueprint of his daddy!** King David tried to move God man's way, and it didn't work and Uzzah's death was the result of that wrong move! Then King David and all of Israel found the ONLY WAY to move God and that was through Blood and Sacrifice! And David shared this with his son, King Solomon, before he died and he shared with him that to move The

Ark of The Covenant it MUST BE THROUGH THE BLOOD COVENANT CEREMONY!

King David was allowed by God to make the preparations to build The Temple (1 Chronicles 23-26, 28:11-19). He bought the land to where The Temple would be built (2 Samuel 24:18-24). God gave David the blueprints and plans on how to build The Temple (1 Chronicles 28:11-19). And King David gave much of the resources to build The Temple (1 Chronicles 22:2-16, 2 Chronicles 5:1). With all that David did to prepare for the building of The Temple, God told him that he couldn't build it for he was a warrior and had shed blood (1 Chronicles 28:2-3). But God <u>did</u> allow his son Solomon to build The Temple for God.

Now, with all that God allowed King David to do and to even giving David the plans on HOW TO BUILD The Temple, don't you think that David TOLD HIS SON HOW TO MOVE THE ARK OF THE COVENANT? *Of course David did! He would not want another failure of transport of The Ark like he experienced!* King David shared ALL that God had given him on how to build The Temple and he also shared with Solomon ALL that he had wisdom about in his time of caring for The Ark in Jerusalem and transporting The Ark to Jerusalem.

Why am I going to great lengths to show you that David and the people of Israel moved The Ark of The Covenant and sacrificed two animals every six paces? Because there are many that believe that King David and the people of Israel would not do such a thing. They are quoted as saying that it is impossible for this large of a sacrifice to occur and just too much of an event to have really happened. It would be too extraordinary to do such a thing is what they believe. The size of the sacrifices and the enormity of the task is impractical and too radical is what they say.

Yet, our God moves in the impractical! Our God does things by faith, not by fact or sight! And our Father had NOT been with His People for many, many years! And He finally had a King that was after His Own Heart and would do what He wanted, and that was to be with His People and the People to be with Him again! I believe that God would give His People extraordinary strength, wisdom and might to bring The Ark of His Covenant back to His City, with strength and might left over to dance, sing and shout all the way there!

Two animals sacrificed every six paces. . . over 30,000 people moving all together in blood. King David accomplished this and he taught his son HOW TO do this also! And King Solomon's radical behavior was even more than his daddy's. *His amount of sacrifice couldn't even be counted or reported when he moved The Ark of The Covenant!*

And we also see that a special sacrifice was done in addition to the "oxen" and "fatted sheep" every six steps! Because God had helped the Levites carry the Ark of The Covenant all that way and with no dilemma (like that of Uzzah), we see another sacrifice of thankfulness to The Lord in 1 Chronicles 15:26 (NIV): *"Because God had helped the Levites who were carrying the ark of the covenant of the LORD, **seven bulls and seven rams were sacrificed.**"* This sacrifice was just a "thank you" that The Lord helped the Levites to carry The Ark all that way, with no problems. Again, supernatural and extraordinary help and strength came from God to do this enormous task that amazing day!

Never Like This!

Now, getting back to The Blood Covenant Ceremony that King David, the Israelites and God's Presence in The Ark of The Covenant were within that day from Obed-edom's house to Jerusalem, this Covenant Ceremony was not like any that had ever been before! **In this Ceremony, the Covenant Site was not just one location; it was on an ongoing path on the roads from Obed-edom's house to the Tent Site in Jerusalem!**

As we just recalled, in a Blood Covenant Ceremony, The Covenant Animal(s) is split down the center, the two halves fall apart and the blood and insides of that Animal flow out into the center of the two pieces of flesh. And remember, if there is more than one Animal for The Blood Covenant, then the additional Animals are lined up *right in front of or behind the other animals.* One animal is placed in front of the other so that when sliced in half, the two halves of flesh form a wall of flesh on each side opposite of each other, with the blood, organs and remaining insides flowing to the center of the two halves of flesh – one animal in front or behind the other!

And in between these two walls of flesh that fall open where the blood, guts and insides of the Covenant Animal lay, THE COVENANT REPRESENTATIVES THEN GO AND STAND AND THEN TAKE THE WALK OF BLOOD BETWEEN THE WALLS OF ANIMAL FLESH! Yet, in this Blood Covenant Ceremony between God, King David and all the Israelites, there was not just one animal, but two animals, a bull and a fattened calf – **EVERY SIX STEPS! And that was EVERY SIX STEPS from Obed-edom's house to the Tent Site for The Ark of The Covenant in Jerusalem!**

Thousands of oxen and sheep cut down the center **making a walkway or alleyway of blood between the two halves of animals!** And seeing approximately 30,000 people all walking, dancing and praising God right down the center of the **walkway of blood!** And of course having so many people participate in this Blood Covenant Ceremony (30,000) helped tremendously in the sacrificing of the Covenant Animals! All of the people of Israel played a part in this Blood Covenant Ceremony – because all were coming into Covenant with God! Thousands of people of Israel rejoicing between the walls of flesh and blood, on those paths all the way to Jerusalem that glorious day. *What an astonishing sight that must have been!* This was one of the largest Blood Covenant Ceremonies in history!

Can we even grasp what this really looked like? David and all The House of Israel and the priests, carrying the Ark of The Covenant, the musicians ALL carrying God (who is one of the Covenant Representatives) through blood and the entrails of Animal Covenant Sacrifices WITH EVERY SIX STEPS THEY MADE from Obed-edom's house to the Tent site located in

Jerusalem! God, inside the Ark of The Covenant, as One Covenant Representative and King David and all the people of Israel (being the other Covenant Representatives) ALL going through the blood continually! **Every six paces was the length of the animals used! It was wall to wall flesh and blood all the way to Jerusalem – making an alley of blood!!!!!!!!**

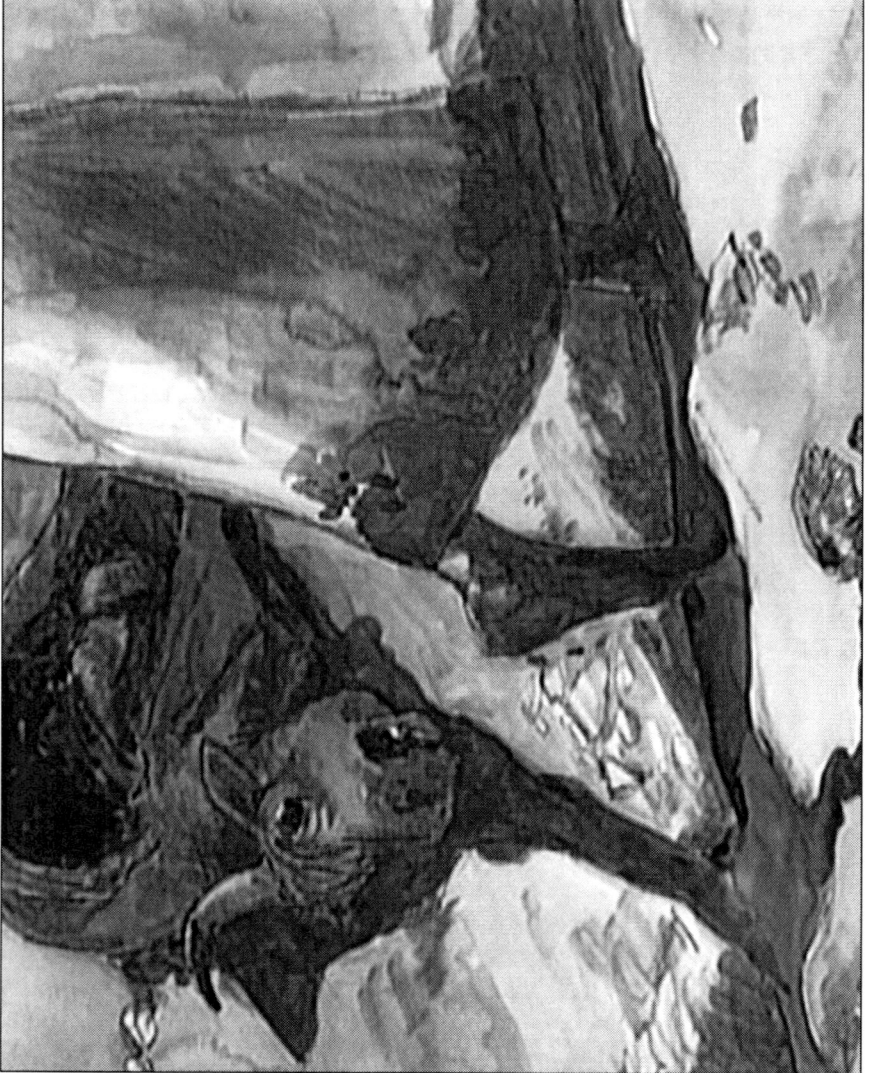

And let's not forget that the Levites and Priests are carrying The Ark of The Covenant, God Himself right through that blood and flesh, too. Therefore, God also would make His Walk of Blood in The Blood Covenant Ceremony! He was the other Covenant Representative here and He was right with The Other Covenant Family, David and the people of Israel, while they were walking within the Walls of Flesh of the Covenant Animals!

King David, the priests and all of Israel walking ankle to knee deep in blood, guts, organs and entrails of this continual wall and alley of Covenant Animals! All of Israel with God coming into Blood Covenant again! Were King David and Israel serious? YOU BETTER BELIEVE IT! They knew that for over 100 years God was not part of their lives or Nation in the way He should have been all along. They wanted God back in their Nation and in Jerusalem and in their lives! So, on this second attempt to come back into Fellowship and Covenant with God, they searched out and finally knew the correct way to enter into Covenant with God, and that was through blood!

Blood and the color of blood – RED – was everywhere! All of Israel and its King and priests dancing, marching, singing and playing instruments – with all of their might – just like their King, David, was doing, all through miles of flesh and blood! In the Jewish Bible Translation it reads:

> *"King David was told, "ADONAI has blessed the house of 'Oved-Edom and everyone who belongs to him, thanks to the ark of God." So David went and <u>joyously</u> brought the ark of God up from the house of 'Oved-Edom into the City of David. 13 When those bearing the ark of ADONAI had gone only six paces, he sacrificed an ox and a fattened sheep. 14 **<u>Then David danced and spun around with abandon before ADONAI,</u>** wearing a linen ritual vest. **<u>15 So David and all the house of Isra'el brought up the ark of ADONAI with shouting and the sound of the shofar.</u>"** 2 Samuel 6:12-15 (Complete Jewish Bible)*

Not only were all of Israel and King David walking through all of the flesh and blood of the Covenant Animals, *but we see that there was dancing and spinning in the flesh and blood, too!* Everything and everyone would have had blood on them and it! Blood, of course, on their feet, ankles, legs, clothing, tambourines and rams' horns! Blood splashed on their arms and faces as they danced and while others around them danced along with King David with total "abandonment!" Flesh on them and others while they spun in the sacrifices moving toward Jerusalem! And blood covering all the people in front and behind them while all were praising God! No one cared what they looked like in the blood and no one cared what they looked like in their praise!

King David even told Michal, his wife, who did not go with him and was judging how David looked and his actions when he arrived back into Jerusalem with The Ark of The Covenant:

". . . I will celebrate before the LORD. 22 I will become even more undignified than this, and I will be humiliated in my own eyes." 2 Samuel 6:21-22 (NIV)

Total freedom and no hindrance from other people and what they thought of you. . . that was a significant element for everyone involved in this special Blood Covenant Ceremony.

I mean, let's think about this! What a sight! Dancing, spinning, rejoicing, shouting—all done with total abandonment of themselves or what they looked like or of the flesh they felt under their feet, or the blood around their legs! They abandoned and neglected to even pay attention to what the ones spinning and dancing in joy in front or behind them looked like in this bloody procession! Nothing was left untouched by the Blood of The Covenant Animals. One Covenant Animal lined up in front of the other, then cut down the center and *all of Israel and King David marching through the blood and flesh. . . all the way to Jerusalem! Amazing!*

King David, the priests and all of Israel would never forget the smells, the sights and what it felt like that Covenant Day, while they made their way through the blood and the literal insides of all those Covenant Animals! If one could have seen this long parade of Covenant coming into town they would have heard shouts, singing, blasts of instruments and *saw approximately 30,000 people dancing and moving about **in a blur of the color red!*** Truly, it was a <u>Walk</u> <u>of</u> <u>Blood</u> during *this* Blood Covenant Ceremony!

No Robe For The King

"<u>Now David was clothed in a robe of fine linen</u>, as were all the Levites who were carrying the ark, and as were the singers, and Kenaniah, who was in charge of the singing of the choirs. David also wore a linen ephod." 1 Chronicles 15:27 (NIV)

And yet we know that in the midst of the Blood Covenant Ceremony that King David disrobed. By the time David and all of Israel walked and praised in the Blood Covenant Ceremony from Obed–edom's house into Jerusalem, he no longer had his robe on!

"Then David returned to bless his household. And [his wife] Michal daughter of Saul came out to meet David and said, <u>How glorious was the king of Israel today, who stripped himself of his kingly robes and uncovered himself</u> in the eyes of his servants' maids as one of the worthless fellows shamelessly uncovers himself!" 2 Samuel 6:20 (AMP)

Still fulfilling another condition of The Blood Covenant Ceremony, King David, the Representative of this Ceremony, praised and sacrificed himself right out of his Robe! Right in the middle of dancing, spinning and abandoning himself in this Walk of Blood, he released and stripped his sign of authority and rank, his robe, and surrendered all of it unto the other Representative of the Blood Covenant, God Himself!

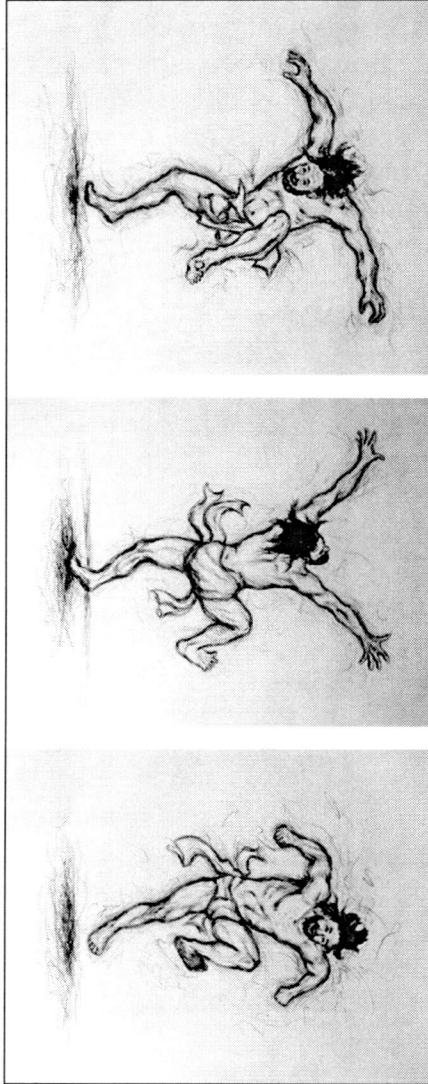

John the Baptist Artworks (JTBA) Artist: Rebecca Brogan

"The Joy of The Redeemed (King David Dancing)
www.jtbarts.com

My Kingship Is Yours!

We must repeat that the Hebrew word "robe" here is OT:4598 *me 'iyl (meh-eel')*, which means *in the sense of covering; a robe (i.e., upper and outer garment): a cloak, coat, mantle, robe.* Just like we have addressed before, when Jonathan, King Saul's son, disrobed within his Blood Covenant Ceremony with David many years before this day of bringing the Ark of God back to Jerusalem, *Jonathan gave David his mantle, his authority.* Jonathan handed to David *his strength, power and authority to become the next King of Israel.*

> 1 Samuel 18:3-4 (AMP) – *"Then Jonathan made **a covenant** with David, because he loved him as his own life. And Jonathan stripped himself of the robe that was on him and gave it to David, and his armor, even his sword, his bow, and his girdle."*

And then in 1 Samuel 23:17-18 (AMP) – *"He said to him, Fear not; the hand of Saul my father shall not find you. You shall be king over Israel, and I shall be next to you. Saul my father knows that too. And the two of them made **a covenant** before the Lord."*

When King David stripped himself of his Kingly Robe he was within the Blood Covenant Ceremony with the other Covenant Representative, God. When David disrobed, it was as if he was saying to God, **"All that I am, all that I have is yours. This position, rank and mantle as King is yours, I give You this position and rank and authority. All my strength and power is yours, God."**

Just like Jonathan relinquished his Kingly Rights to David, therefore giving him the "legal" right to be the King of Israel, David did the same to God that day during The Blood Covenant Ceremony! Revelation 5:5 (NLT) tells us:

"But one of the twenty-four elders said to me, "Stop weeping! Look, the Lion of the tribe of Judah, **the heir to David's throne,** *has won the victory. He is worthy to open the scroll and its seven seals."*

And in Revelation 22:16 (NLT), *"I, Jesus, have sent my angel to give you this message for the churches.* **I am both the source of David and the heir to his throne.** *I am the bright morning star."*

John the Baptist Artworks (JTBA)

Artist: Rebecca Brogan

"The Lion of Judah Reigns" **www.jtbarts.com**

King David "stripped" his "Kingly Robe" of authority that Blood Covenant Day and gave God the right to lawfully make King Jesus, God's First Born, the Everlasting King and Heir to David's Throne! If you are an "heir" you have been given something and it has willfully been handed over to you. King David made Jesus The Heir to his throne.

*". . . and the throne of David shall be established before the L*ORD *forever." 1 Kings 2:45 (KJV)*

A legal and spiritual "transaction" occurred between Jonathan and David that day during the Blood Covenant Ceremony that they shared. Jonathan, the "one to be next to have the throne" within the Blood Covenant Ceremony, *disrobed his authority to be the next King of Israel and gave his robe and authority and title to David!* Again, let's look at The Word:

1 Samuel 18:3-4 (AMP) – *"Then Jonathan made* ***a covenant*** *with David, because he loved him as his own life. And Jonathan stripped himself of the robe that was on him and gave it to David, and his armor, even his sword, his bow, and his girdle."*

And then in 1 Samuel 23:17-18 (AMP) – *". . . You shall be king over Israel, and I shall be next to you. Saul my father knows that too. And the two of them made* ***a covenant*** *before the Lord."*

Jonathan then states as one of the Conditions of this Blood Covenant, while standing in Blood with David, that he (David) shall be the King of Israel! Jonathan gave David his robe in one Blood Covenant Ceremony and then states the results of that action in another Blood Covenant Ceremony. Jonathan made it very clear by the giving of his robe, which is his title, mantle and authority, what he was coming into Covenant with

David about. *He was handing over his Kingship!* And it would only be acceptable and binding through The Blood Covenant!

And so we see King David disrobing <u>himself</u> of his title, his position, his rank and his authority! Taking now <u>his</u> Kingly Robe, completely drenched in blood and stripping himself in a Blood Covenant! Can you see it in your mind? The one that God Himself chose to sit over His People Israel, coming through all of the Blood of all of those Covenant Animals, all to come into a Blood Covenant with God Almighty!

Yes, King David, all the people of Israel and Father God were coming into Covenant that day, and yet the disrobing of King David was very public and very private. King David and all of Israel were the *Covenant Representatives* that day. All were within the blood and coming into Covenant with each other and God. And when King David *publicly* took off his robe, he and all of Israel were letting God know that all of their titles and authority and strength were now His. King David and all of Israel were committing themselves in blood to Father God and were now in Covenant with Him that they would fight His battles and would come when He needed them. This was what David's *public* disrobing meant for himself and all of Israel. And let's not forget that God, Himself was being transported in the blood too! All Covenant Representatives, God, Israel and King David were in blood, for you know that blood was splashed onto The Ark during The Walk of Blood! All together, all coming into Covenant and all Representatives of The Covenant covered in blood!

It's All In The Family!

And yet King David's *private* disrobing meant a whole other thing for him. For David knew well how *he was lawfully made the King of Israel. . . by two families joining together by Blood Covenant!* **The rightful heir to the King of Israel, King Saul, had to lay down <u>his</u> Robe or Mantle within a Blood Covenant Ceremony with David. . .** and God knew that King Saul would never do that **so Jonathan, the son of King Saul, did just that.** When Jonathan gave up his throne and gave it to David through the Blood Covenant Ceremony that he performed with David, **Jonathan not only made the way for David to be the King of Israel, he also made the initial way for Jesus, the Heir of David, to become The King of Israel, too!**

King David is now within a Blood Covenant Ceremony, covered in blood, and he disrobes himself before God personally, signifying that he gives all his titles and authority to God. In order for the First Born of Father God, Jesus, to be the rightful heir to King David's throne as prophesied by Nathan in 2 Samuel 7:16 (AMP), *"And your house and your kingdom shall be made sure forever before you; your throne shall be established forever,"* **Jesus would have to become a part of Saul's family, the first King of Israel.**

See, Jesus was and is an Heir to King David not only through his earthly father Joseph and his earthly mother Mary; He is also the Son of Father God, which King David is now coming into Covenant with through blood! Joseph and Mary BOTH were in the bloodline of David physically and because David himself came into Blood Covenant with Father God, Jesus rightfully was able to become and continually be The Eternal King of Israel on His Heavenly Father's side of the family too! Leaving no doubt whose family and lineage Jesus came through, because King David and Father God merged their families together in The Blood Covenant that day, allowing Jesus to come through David's natural family and still yet remain God's family! And it was executed and carried out on Earth and in Heaven through Father God and King David and through blood!

Remember, **David was not a part of the family of King Saul! Blood Covenant MADE HIM FAMILY THROUGH JONATHAN! David was not in line to be The King of Israel. BLOOD COVENANT MADE HIM IN LINE TO BE THE KING! And just like King David was given the Mantle or Robe to become the "heir" of The King of Israel through Jonathan,**

Jesus would have to receive the Mantle or Robe from A King of Israel. He would have to receive it from A King of Israel to BE AN HEIR! Someone had to "heir" the throne of Israel to God and His family and King David did it that day during The Blood Covenant Ceremony!

The word "heir" means, "one who inherits or is entitled to succeed to a hereditary rank, title, or office." **When King David disrobed, he gave Father God (The Other Covenant Representative) his title of King of Israel, and another Heir would now be able to receive David's throne, just like it was given to him through Jonathan. David gave his rights to the throne to another.** And God gave the title, rank and office of The King of Israel to His First Born, Jesus.

". . . and the throne of David shall be established before the LORD forever." 1Kings 2:45 (KJV)

And it could only be through Covenant and the merging of two families – the families of David and Father God! And it could only be through **Blood! And oh, how much blood there was to usher in Jesus, the "Heir" to The Throne of The King of Israel, Who Is and shall always be on David's Throne and David's Heir. . . every six paces blood was shed all the way from Obed-edom's house to Jerusalem!** *Remember, God will always do everything in order and will always follow "protocol", too!*

We've Arrived!

When King David and all the people of Israel arrived in Jerusalem with The Ark of The Covenant, they still entered the City celebrating and praising God! They had walked for miles, sacrificing Covenant Animals and praising God through the Walk of Blood all the way to Jerusalem. And still, when King David arrived he set The Ark in its place that he had prepared for God and then made more sacrifices of burnt offerings and peace offerings To The Lord in thankfulness for what God had helped him and the people do that day!

> *"They brought the Ark of the Lord and set it in its place inside the special tent David had prepared for it. And David sacrificed burnt offerings and peace offerings to the Lord. 18 When he had finished his sacrifices, David blessed the people in the name of the Lord of Heaven's Armies. 19 Then he gave to every Israelite man and woman in the crowd a loaf of bread, a cake of dates, and a cake of raisins. Then all the people returned to their homes."* 2 Samuel 6:17-19 (NLT)

This sounds very much like what we know that King Solomon did. The Bible tells us that when he arrived at The New Temple from moving The Ark, he sacrificed to The Lord at the Temple, in addition to what he had sacrificed while moving The Ark. *Again, he learned that from his father David.*

Yet there is one last aspect of The Blood Covenant Ceremony that we see happening here between King David and the people of God, and that is **The Covenant Meal.** The Bible says:

> *"When he had finished his sacrifices, David blessed the people in the name of the Lord of Heaven's Armies.* **19 *Then he gave to every Israelite man and woman in the crowd a loaf of bread, a cake of dates, and a cake of raisins.*** *Then all the people returned to their homes."* 2 Sam. 6:18-19 (NLT)

Not only was there great extravagance in the many sacrifices all the way from Obed-edom's house to Jerusalem, we see here King David giving every man and woman *a loaf of bread, a cake of dates, and a cake of raisins.* Now, remember we know that there were at the very least 30,000 people within this Blood Covenant Ceremony. Just that number would be nearly 100,000 cakes or loaves of bread! But that is one of the significant parts of The Blood Covenant Ceremony, and that is to share food with each other through your Covenant!

Truly, King David and the people of Israel fulfilled The Blood Covenant Ceremony with God!

The Covenant Representatives *(Father God in The Ark and King David and The People of Israel)*

The Covenant Sites were Chosen *(the roads and paths from Obed-edom's house to Jerusalem)*

Conditions of Covenant were decided on and declared, Promises Proclaimed *(Conditions in The Ark, and all that King David Proclaimed while in Jerusalem when The Ark Arrived)*

Animal(s) were Cut *(thousands of oxen and sheep on the way to Jerusalem and 7 bulls upon arrival to Jerusalem)*

Walk of Blood *(King David and at least 30,000 people of Israel all walking, dancing and rejoicing in the blood to Jerusalem)*

Giving of Coats *(David gave his Coat, His Robe and his throne to God that day)*

Covenant Meal *(Thousands now in the Covenant together shared, bread, and cakes of dates and raisins.)*

What an astounding example of how serious God is about Blood Covenant and how valuable His People are to Him! And what an astounding example of just how much God's People will do to be with Him, too!

Chapter Ten

You Were Always On My Mind

🌰

"AND DAVID said, Is there still anyone left of the house
of Saul to whom I may show kindness for Jonathan's sake?"
2 Samuel 9:1 (AMP)

*J*onathan was always beside the King of Israel, whether it be his father, King Saul, or the future King, David. He knew that David was to be the next King of Israel and at their Second Covenant Ceremony, Jonathan stated that he would be beside David. Had Jonathan followed David and left his father's side, he would have been put in authority beside his Covenant brother and friend in David's kingdom.

Many years later, after Jonathan has died and David is now The King of Israel, we find a wonderful example of what a Blood Covenant really means. As a partaker of a Blood Covenant with another, the Covenant is forever to be on ones' mind.

We find that one day David is remembering his Covenant Promises that he made with Jonathan. And what did King David want to do? He wanted to uphold the promises that he made to Jonathan. How does one do that when Jonathan is

134

dead? Remember that in the Blood Covenant Ceremony it goes on for generations and generation. . . forever!

That is why there are normally witnesses to the Covenant Ceremony, so that the Covenant Promises will carry on from generation to generation due to witnesses who heard the Covenant Promises and saw the steps that were taken by the Covenant Representatives of the two families coming together, and then this is passed on for generations and generations, forever. Since the Covenant Cut between David and Jonathan was only witnessed by the two of them, David, being the only one alive, would carry the weight of the Blood Covenant.

King David had his Covenants that he made with Jonathan on his mind.

1 Samuel 18:3-4 (AMP) – *"Then Jonathan made **a covenant** with David, because he loved him as his own life. And Jonathan stripped himself of the robe that was on him and gave it to David, and his armor, even his sword, his bow, and his girdle."*

I'd imagine that he was remembering the Covenant Animal that was cut and the blood that came from that animal. David would recall the blood that he and Jonathan stood in as the Covenant Representatives professing their Covenant Promises that they would forever keep to each other and their families.

David would recollect and maybe even hold in his hands the belt, the girdle, the bow, the armor and the sword that his Covenant brother and friend, Jonathan, had given him that day during the Covenant. And just looking at himself now, sitting on the throne, and all the possessions that he now has because Jonathan gave him *his* right to be The King of Israel, I'm sure just overtook him! And when the memories and weight of the Blood Covenant Ceremonies and blessings that he now had because of Jonathan overwhelmed him, David bellowed out of his soul!

"One day David asked, "Is anyone in Saul's family still alive—anyone to whom I can show kindness for Jonathan's sake?" 2 He summoned a man named Ziba, who had been one of Saul's servants. "Are you Ziba?" the king asked. "Yes sir, I am," Ziba replied. 3 The king then asked him, "Is anyone still alive from Saul's family? If so, I want to show God's kindness to them." Ziba replied, "Yes, one of Jonathan's sons is still alive. He is crippled in both feet." 4 "Where is he?" the king asked. "In Lo-debar," Ziba told him, "at the home of Makir son of Ammiel."

5 So David sent for him and brought him from Makir's home. 6 His name was Mephibosheth; he was Jonathan's son and Saul's grandson. When he came to David, he bowed low to the ground in deep respect. David said, "Greetings, Mephibosheth." Mephibosheth replied, "I am your servant." 7 "Don't be afraid!" David said. "I intend to show kindness to you because of my promise to your father, Jonathan. I will give you all the property that once belonged to your grandfather Saul, and you will eat here with me at the king's table!"

8 Mephibosheth bowed respectfully and exclaimed, "Who is your servant, that you should show such kindness to a dead dog like me?" 9 Then the king summoned Saul's servant Ziba and said, "I have given your master's grandson everything that belonged to Saul and his family. 10 You and your sons and servants are to farm the land for him to produce food for your master's household. But Mephibosheth, your master's grandson, will eat here at my table." (Ziba had fifteen sons and twenty servants.)

11 Ziba replied, "Yes, my lord the king; I am your servant, and I will do all that you have commanded." And from that time on, Mephibosheth ate regularly at David's table, like one of the king's own sons. 12 Mephibosheth had a young son named Mica. From then on, all the members of Ziba's household were Mephibosheth's servants. 13 And Mephibosheth, who was crippled in both feet, lived in Jerusalem and ate regularly at the king's table." 2 Samuel 9:1-13 (NLT)

What A Difference A Day Makes

"Saul's son Jonathan had a son named Mephibosheth, who was crippled as a child. He was five years old when the report came from Jezreel that Saul and Jonathan had been killed in battle. When the child's nurse heard the news, she picked him up and fled. But as she hurried away, she dropped him, and he became crippled."
2 Samuel 4:4 (NLT)

Mephibosheth's life changed drastically that day. He went from being the grandson of the King to being urgently taken to save his life from the enemies that wanted to destroy Saul's Kingdom and his "would-be" heirs to the throne. His nurse was to guard little Mephibosheth's life and in the midst of fleeing, since the word had arrived that Mephibosheth's father Jonathan and grandfather King Saul were now dead, she dropped him. Mephibosheth was now crippled in not just one but many ways in his life.

Mephibosheth woke up one day in Lo-debar (which means "no pasture," "no word," and "no communication") and within minutes, his whole life would again change. Mephibosheth was in Lo-debar where there looked like no hope for prosperity or "pasture" or the good land for him and his family. Mephibosheth was receiving no "good news" or "word" or "communication" about his situation while residing in "Lo-debar."

Born into the royal family, grandson of King Saul and the son of Jonathan, Mephibosheth now was limited due to being crippled in his feet and the restrictedness that living in Lo-debar brought. With the Kingdom of Saul now faded, Mephibosheth was limited for now, without the aid of a family and the servants and assistance he needed. Life at Lo-debar was indeed low. Lo-debar was not only Mephibosheth's address, it was his condition of belief in God and hope for his future. For later he calls himself "a dead dog like me." (2 Samuel 9:8) Mephibosheth couldn't see goodness in the land of his life and he was in a place of Lo-debar, where he couldn't hear God's voice or Word and His promises for his future.

Then one day. . . a day like none other in Mephibosheth's life came. The day The Blood Covenant that his father, Jonathan had with now King David was so heavily on King David's mind that he couldn't ignore it any longer. The day that David sent for Mephibosheth because of The Blood Covenant that had been Cut between him and Jonathan—yes, this day would change everything for Mephibosheth!

The day had come that all of Mephibosheth's and his son's needs would be met! The day had finally come when Mephibosheth moved from having no hope and no word in Lo-debar to the royal setting of the King's Palace! The day had arrived that Mephibosheth went from having no "pasture" in Lo-debar to having his grandfather King Saul's land given to him and servants to tend to it and bring him the produce from it (2 Samuel 9:10)!

On this day ALL his needs would forever be met by King David, and why all of this turnaround? Because A Blood Covenant was Cut, not by Mephibosheth, but by his father! Blood Covenant is forever and is forever set in the families! Mephibosheth means "shame destroyer" and "image breaker." How wonderful it is that The Blood Covenant Cut between David and Jonathan not only broke the shame that Mephibosheth was carrying for so many years, but the image that he had of himself and his future was now "broken" and totally made new!

Mephibosheth's image was now of hope, provision and freedom for him and his son! So many lives made whole and prosperous and blessed–Mephibosheth's, his family's, Ziba's and all of his families. . . all due to a Blood Covenant made many years prior. Blood Covenants are forever and for generations! Think about Mephibosheth and how because of a Covenant his life changed in just one day. God can take you too friend from Lo-debar to the King's castle and the King's provision and goodness. I pray that for you. That you friend, move right now from Lo-debar to the King's table and Lord I ask You to do this for my friend reading this, in just one day in Jesus Name!

Chapter Eleven

NOT ONCE, BUT TWICE

". . . they could not be recorded or counted."
1 Kings 8:5 (NIV)

We have thoroughly detailed The Blood Covenant Ceremonies that took place in King David's life and even how they connect with us. And we have also mentioned in part the Blood Covenant Ceremony that King David's son, King Solomon, experienced and how it related to King David's. We must look a little deeper into the magnificent splendor and holiness that took place on that wonderful day of The Blood Covenant Ceremony that King Solomon conducted, for there is more to unveil!

Solomon had been selected by God to build Him a Place, a Temple. What a privilege and what an assignment! And as we had said before, King David really wanted to build God a Place, but God told him his son Solomon would. We had written earlier that King David had his hands on much of the preparation of this Temple for God.

King David was allowed by God to make the preparations to build The Temple (1 Chronicles 23-26, 28:11-19). He bought the land where The Temple would be built (2 Samuel 24:18-24). God gave David the blueprints and plans on how to build The Temple (1 Chronicles 28:11-19). And King David gave much of the resources to build The Temple and the sacred articles of it (1 Chronicles 22:2-16, 2 Chronicles 5:1). With all that David did to prepare for the building of The Temple, God told him that he couldn't build it for he was a warrior and had shed blood (1 Chronicles 28:2-3).

Now, with all that God allowed King David to do in preparing The Temple, David also gave his son, Solomon the wisdom that he had and the directions God had given him on how to build The Temple and of course, how to move God, The Ark, into The Temple. And King David knew that the ONLY WAY was to do it through The Blood Covenant Ceremony. Again, The Blood Covenant Ceremony is and has always been throughout The Word of God, and it has always been God's Way! We see that The Word tells us that King Solomon really did take heed and follow his daddy's directions.

"Solomon loved the Lord, walking [at first] in the statutes and practices of David his father,. . ." 1 Kings 3:3 (AMP)

King Solomon followed the very *blueprint of King David's movement of The Ark of The Covenant* and *this* Blood Covenant Ceremony may have been even greater and more extravagant than his father's!

The Covenant Representatives are chosen for this historical day of The Temple and of Covenant! The Blood Covenant Representatives are King Solomon and the elders of Israel, all the heads of the Tribes and the Chiefs of all the Israelite families.

"Then King Solomon summoned into his presence at Jerusalem the elders of Israel, all the heads of the tribes and the chiefs of the Israelite families, to bring up the ark of the LORD's covenant from Zion, the City of David. 2 All the men of Israel came together to King Solomon at the time of the festival in the month of Ethanim, the seventh month." 1 Kings 8:1-2 (NIV)

And "all the men of Israel" are also present for this Covenant Ceremony, for it was the time of The Feast of Tabernacles in Jerusalem! So thousands of people would have been there at this time of year, for Israel was commanded to pilgrimage to Jerusalem during this Feast!

". . . you shall keep the Feast of Ingathering [Booths or Tabernacles] at the end of the year, when you gather in the fruit of your labors from the field. 17 Three times in the year all your males shall appear before the Lord God." Exodus 23:16-17 (AMP)

So not only would have Israel's elders, heads of Tribes and Chief family Representatives been at this Blood Covenant Ceremony, *practically all of Israel and all those who had traveled to Israel for The Feast of Tabernacles* would have been there, also! And all would have the opportunity to come into this Blood Covenant, too! The entire City of Jerusalem would have been overflowing with people, all celebrating the harvest time and now, celebrating that God was being placed in their very own Temple!

The Covenant Site was chosen and it, too, like David's Blood Covenant Ceremony, would have been mobile from the "Tent" or "Tabernacle" that King David had erected to put The Ark of The Covenant in to The Temple. The Blood Covenant Ceremony would begin in The City of David, through the streets of Jerusalem and to The Temple, now built, and finally resting within *The Holy of Holies* within The Temple.

The Conditions of The Covenant and Promises Proclaimed were, of course, within The Ark of The Covenant that God Himself was coming into Covenant with the people in. Along with all The Covenant Conditions He had given to His People through the prior Covenants made through Abraham, Moses, the Hebrew Children and King David, all Covenant Conditions were coming together. Covenant Conditions were proclaimed vocally by King Solomon himself. Solomon cried out before The Lord with great petitions and Promises on behalf of himself and the Nation of Israel. And you can find them in 1 Kings 8:14-61, where he was speaking them and reverently kneeling before the altar with his hands raised in worship.

"When Solomon finished making these prayers and petitions to the LORD, <u>he stood up in front of the altar of the LORD, where he had been kneeling with his hands raised toward heaven</u>." 1 Kings 8:54-55 (NLT)

The Covenant Animal was Cut and *cut and cut and cut!* As we have discussed before, King Solomon followed his father's directions and wisdom on HOW TO MOVE The Ark of The Covenant. As a matter of fact, you can clearly see that Solomon followed HOW David did the WHOLE COVENANT CEREMONY! And one thing truly mirrored by Solomon concerning David's Ceremony *was the extreme amount of Blood that was present! Covenant Animals were Cut everywhere to bring The Ark of The Covenant in!*

*"When all the elders of Israel had arrived, the priests took up the ark, 4 and they brought up the ark of the LORD and the Tent of Meeting and all the sacred furnishings in it. **The priests and Levites <u>carried them up</u>, 5 and King Solomon and the entire assembly of Israel that had <u>gathered about him</u> were <u>before the ark</u>, SACRIFICING SO MANY SHEEP AND CATTLE THAT THEY COULD NOT BE RECORDED OR COUNTED.**"* 1 Kings 8:3-5 (NIV)

And I know that we have gone over this, but it must be brought out once more! The significance of this is huge! King Solomon led all the Leaders and Elders and *all the people of Israel* and *all the people in Jerusalem for The Feast,* and here he comes with all of these people *(I'm sure thousands, because that is what his daddy did)* through the streets of Jerusalem! And he and these thousands of people are *in front, before The Ark of The Covenant,* and Covenant Animals are being Covenant Cut one right after the other alongside them. Remember, when using more than one Covenant Animal you place them alongside each other, making a "Walkway" or "Alleyway" by Cutting them so that they are in **halves for people to walk through!** Keeping in mind, Covenant in the Hebrew is the word, *beriyth (ber-eeth')* OT:1285, **a compact made by passing between pieces of flesh: covenant, league. To cut, To divide.**

And King Solomon and all of the Leadership and the People of Israel are praising God, dancing, clapping, spinning and praising God, *just like David and the People of God did when The Ark arrived in Jerusalem!* And let's not forget that the Levites and Priests are carrying The Ark, God, right through that blood, too, making God also make His Walk of Blood in The Blood Covenant Ceremony!

Everyone is walking through the centers of these Cut Covenant Animals, and they are celebrating right through the entrails of these Animals, all displaying love for God between the Walls of Flesh and "Alleyways" of The Blood Covenant! There is so much blood, no one can even count how many Covenant Animals there are or how many they even brought to sacrifice!

And there is so much blood, so much excitement and jubilation, **that no one cares how many there are! Counting The Covenant Animals is not what's on their minds!** Celebrating God, celebrating the Harvest Time, celebrating The Feast, celebrating The Temple of God. . . and all the People are in a parade of thankfulness and love for God and in a parade of *blood!*

I'd imagine that those who didn't even know that The Blood Covenant Ceremony was going to be taking place when they arrived in Jerusalem for The Feast joined right in on the Ceremony right from the "sidewalks" or "side ways" and began dancing and celebrating right in the midst of the blood and flesh of the Covenant Animals *that couldn't even be counted,* right along with everyone else!

All present would know what was going on when they witnessed this great sight. See, at this time in history Blood Covenant Ceremonies were not unknown, like today. The People of God knew of their Promises of God and the people knew Blood Covenant is how they got them. Even the males as babies are a part of a Blood Covenant through circumcision. So to see This Blood Covenant Ceremony taking place and all can join in and partake. . . well, that's about the best day ever when you really know that it is joining you with another family. . . and that Family is God's!

King Solomon followed his daddy's directions on the details of building The Temple and this Ceremony. I'd also imagine that many talks and intimate discussions took place between David and his son.

Son, a Covenant always has to have Blood! I tried so hard to move The Ark of God without blood and Uzzah died and his blood was sacrificed! There is life in the Blood. Always remember that, Solomon. For others to live, Blood must be given. The day I and all of Israel came into Blood Covenant with God and moved The Ark to Jerusalem, thousands of animals were sacrificed. The sacrifices were every six paces during the transport. The Blood is what allowed us all to Live as we moved God that second time! This is the most important part of The Temple, my Son. Blood is what moves God.

Years ago, I asked The Lord why when a woman becomes pregnant, her menstrual cycle stops. A few weeks later, God spoke to me and said, *"There's always a sacrifice of blood for life."* At the time, I thought, *Me not having my menstrual cycle would not be a sacrifice; for me, that would be great!* After a time of praying, I realized what The Master was saying to me. For someone to *live* there must be a sacrifice, *a giving up, a substitute of one thing for another,* and for life, it is blood. A woman "sacrifices" her flow of blood so that the baby and life in her may live. *For life is in the blood (Leviticus 17:11).*

Why was there such elation in all the people during this Ceremony of Blood? Because of The Blood Covenant they all realize that they are receiving LIFE (In The Blood)! The Goodness of LIFE (In The Blood), The Blessing of LIFE (In The Blood), The Promises of God in LIFE (In The Blood), The Prosperity of LIFE (In The Blood). . . ALL within The Blood Covenant Ceremony that is taking place right before their eyes! More LIFE and Goodness is being added to them! The Blood Covenant Animals' Blood was making a way for them and their families and families' families to all RECEIVE LIFE – and *Life More Abundantly!*

King Solomon was the Covenant Representative for all the people of God that day. Covered in blood, just like his father, David was, Solomon proclaimed many promises on behalf of the people that were present and the ones to come in the future. What a worshipful day unto God!

Too Much!

Then we see as The Blood Covenant continues, Solomon and all the people arrive at The Temple Site and we see still yet another factor that King Solomon mirrored from his father.

> *"15 So <u>David</u> and <u>all the house of Israel</u> brought up the ark of the LORD with shouting and with the sound of the trumpet. . . . So they brought the ark of the LORD, and set it in its place in the midst of the tabernacle that David had erected for it. **Then David offered burnt offerings and peace offerings before the LORD."***
> 2 Samuel 6:15,17 (NKJV)

And then we see Solomon arriving at his final Covenant Site, and he also offers even MORE sacrifices to dedicate The Place of The Ark of The Covenant.

*"And the king and all Israel with him offered sacrifice before the Lord. 63 **Solomon offered as peace offerings to the Lord: 22,000 oxen and 120,000 sheep.** So **the king and all the Israelites dedicated the house of the Lord.**"* 1 Kings 8:62-63 (AMP)

Now, we must remember that this is a **separate set of sacrifices** from when Solomon is moving The Ark. In that procession there was so much that it could not be counted or recorded! Yet, we see again, Solomon following his father's lead.

*"Because God had helped the Levites who were carrying the ark of the covenant of the LORD, **seven bulls and seven rams were sacrificed.**"* 1 Chronicles 15:26 (NIV)

King David had seven bulls sacrificed when they all arrived in Jerusalem with The Ark of The Covenant. This sacrifice was separate from the sacrifices that had been going on every six steps from Obed-edom's house to Jerusalem!

But what really helps us to picture in our minds this Blood Covenant Ceremony is this next verse.

*"On that same day the king consecrated the **middle part of the courtyard** in front of the temple of the LORD, and there he offered burnt offerings, grain offerings and the fat of the fellowship offerings, **because the bronze altar before the LORD was too small to hold the burnt offerings,** the grain offerings and the fat of the fellowship offerings."* 1Kings 8:64 (NIV)

Let's look at this. The Bible says that there were so many Covenant Animals sacrificed for the people to walk through that day of Covenant in Jerusalem that they could not count them! And we know that King David had sacrifices happening every six steps, and that was from Obed-edom's house to

Jerusalem. Solomon did not have as far to move The Ark as David. Solomon only went from one part of Jerusalem to another and yet the Covenant Animals could not be counted.

And now, we see that King Solomon had to consecrate the middle part of the Courtyard at The Temple, because the Bronze Altar was too small to hold The Burnt Offerings *that were numbered (22,000 cattle and 120,000 sheep and goats and grain offerings and the fat of the fellowship offerings)! Again, this is a separate offering of sacrifices than what they were doing as they were moving The Ark of The Covenant!*

The Blood Covenant Ceremony was HUGE that day in Jerusalem! The procession of Covenant Representatives was HUGE! The praise of God and The Walk of Blood was HUGE! Even the dedication and additional offering to The Lord at The Temple was HUGE! King David absolutely trained Solomon well on how to do a Blood Covenant Ceremony and how to move God!

Pleasing To Him

Let's look at one last thing about this particular Blood Covenant Ceremony that just astounds me! We find that after Solomon and all the people arrive at The Temple after they have all taken their Walk of Blood as Covenant Representatives through all of those Covenant Animals to get there, The Priests take The Ark into The Holy of Holies.

*"King Solomon and all the congregation of Israel who had assembled before him were with him before the ark, sacrificing sheep and oxen, so many that they could not be reported or counted. **6 And the priests brought the ark of the covenant of the Lord to its place in the Holy of Holies of the house, under the wings of the cherubim. 7 <u>For the cherubim spread forth their two wings over the place of the ark, and the cherubim covered the ark and its poles.</u> 8 The***

*poles were so long that the ends of them were seen from the Holy Place before the Holy of Holies, but they were not seen outside; they are there to this day. 9 There was nothing in the ark except the two tables of stone which Moses put there at Horeb, where the Lord made a covenant with the Israelites when they came out of the land of Egypt. 10 When the priests had come out of the Holy Place, **the cloud** filled the Lord's house, 11 So the priests could not stand to minister because of the cloud, for the glory of the Lord had filled the Lord's house."* 1 Kings 8:5-11 (AMP)

The cherubim on The Ark moved! They spread their wings and covered The Ark and the poles like a "canopy" (New Living Translation) or a "tent" that stretched into the Holy Place outside of the Holy of Holies, which is the next room. These cherubim were made out of gold! And yet God showed Himself in this amazing act and made a "Tent" with the wings of the gold cherubim! Wow!

Now, the cherubim making like a "canopy" or "tent" covering the Ark and Poles is key, because The Ark of The Covenant has always, until this very day with Solomon, been within a Tent or Tabernacle. It had started with Moses and the Hebrew Children in the desert. And the very Covenant Tablets that were given in that Blood Covenant Ceremony were still to be found in The Ark on this day! *(It is to be assumed that the Rod of Aaron and the Jar of Manna were taken by the Philistines in The Ark's time of captivity.)*

And we also see that what happened on Mt. Sinai during that Blood Covenant Ceremony also happened at this Blood Covenant Ceremony with Solomon.

*"**On the day** the tabernacle, **the Tent of the Testimony, was set up**, the **cloud** covered it. From evening till morning **the cloud above the tabernacle looked like fire.**"* Numbers 9:15 (NIV)

And we've also seen in this Blood Covenant that Solomon led:

"When the priests had come out of the Holy Place, **the cloud filled the Lord's house,** *11 So* <u>the priests could not stand</u> *to minister because of the cloud, for* **the glory of the Lord had filled the Lord's house."**
1 Kings 8:10-11 (AMP)

Now what is significant here is that God showed up at both of these Blood Covenant Ceremonies and both on the Day they were dedicated or set up! He and The Glory of His Presence was so powerful that He filled The Tabernacle or Tent *and* He filled The Temple. And no one could do anything inside of The Tent or The Temple on their Covenant Days, for The Cloud, God, was just overwhelming! God was pleased with The Places at both! God was so present at this Blood Covenant Ceremony that The Bible says that the ministers could not even stand! God's Power was so strong that the ministers were on the floor and could not get up, they could not stand! Praise The Lord!

When God showed Himself by moving and making a "Tent" over The Ark and the poles, in The Temple, He was pleased with the movement and transport and He was pleased with "the Poles," the way He was moved. He was pleased with The Blood Covenant Ceremony, and it fulfilled His Protocol! He would have never "showed up" if He wasn't pleased. And we see that the Cloud also looked like Fire at The Tent or Tabernacle of Moses. And we know that while dedicating The Temple there was a burnt offering going on that was so big that they had to move it to the Courtyard! Both Fire and The Cloud, which is God at the Tabernacle or Tent of Moses and at The Temple that Solomon built.

And there was so much in Covenant Animals and Harvest at This Feast of Tabernacles during Solomon's Blood Covenant Ceremony that The Bible says that all the people stayed in Jerusalem and celebrated it for **14 days!**

Normally The Feast of Tabernacles lasts for seven days, but there was so much provision for all the people, they stayed another week! Therefore, all the people had many **Covenant Meals together after the Blood Ceremonies!** Therefore, fulfilling this segment of The Blood Covenant Ceremony!

And how appropriate that through this Fall Feast, which means to "dwell" and "tabernacle" with God, that the people did just that those 14 days. God showed Himself just like He did when He "Tabernacled" with the Hebrew Children through the Cloud and the Fire! And The Blood Covenant Ceremony is what enabled it all!

Chapter Twelve

Promise of A King and The People

🌿

"The king stood [on the platform] by the pillar and made a covenant before the Lord-. . ."
2 Kings 23:3 (AMP)

We find in The Word another King who found himself right in the center of a Blood Covenant. In 2 Kings 22-23 we read about a wonderful King named Josiah. Josiah had a very unusual beginning. He came from a royal line of men who did *evil* in the sight of The Lord as they ruled and reigned, and only a very few did what was right in God's eyes. His father, King Amon, was killed during his reign by the servants in his Kingdom. He was succeeded by his son, Josiah.

King Josiah was *eight years old* when he began his reign as King of Judah! And although he had not seen it for himself in those very short eight years of his life through his father or the legacies of other Kings before him, Josiah did what was right before the eyes of The Lord.

Throughout Israel's history we find that many generations did not follow God and did not follow what He said to do and how He said to do it! When King Josiah had arrived at his eighteenth year of reigning, he was having The House of The Lord repaired. And during this time the High Priest of The House of

God found the Book of The Law! (This lets us know that The House of God was not using God's Law to run it, because it was just found! <u>The Church Leaders were running God's House on their own ideas and ideas of those before them!</u>)

The Book of The Law that was found was read to King Josiah and when he heard what God said, he rent or tore his clothes, for he was in great distress. King Josiah knew the Nation was not doing what God had said to do.

King Josiah was dismayed about how the Nation had moved from what God commanded His People to do.

> *"The king went up to the house of the Lord, and with him all the men of Judah, all the inhabitants of Jerusalem, the priests, the prophets, and all the people, both small and great. And **he read in their ears all the words of the Book of the Covenant,** which was <u>found</u> in the Lord's house. 3 **The king stood [on the platform] by the pillar and <u>made a covenant before the Lord</u>**–to walk after the Lord and to keep His commandments, His testimonies, and His statutes with all his heart and soul, to confirm the words of this covenant that were written in this book. **And all the people stood to join in the <u>covenant</u>.***" 2 Kings 23:2-3 (AMP)

Again, we see the Hebrew the word "covenant" here in verses 2 and 3 is *beriyth (ber-eeth')* OT:1285, **a compact made by passing between pieces of flesh: covenant, league. To cut, To divide.** So we know that a Covenant Animal was Cut in half and there was a passing between those two halves of "flesh."

King Josiah had an Animal to be Cut that day, for The Word says he "made a covenant" (*beriyth*). Also, The Bible says that they read The Book of The Covenant, which would have been the first Books of The Bible, and that is where you learn so much about The Blood Covenant Ceremony. Of course, when The King read *from The Book of The Covenant* he would <u>do what</u> <u>he</u> <u>read</u>!

That day all of the Covenant Family gathered. *"The king went up to the house of the Lord, and with him all the men of Judah, all the inhabitants of Jerusalem, the priests, the prophets, and all the people, both small and great."* King Josiah was the Representative of the Covenant Family that was present before God. The King called all the people to watch and hear the terms of The Blood Covenant that were being committed to and read aloud between King Josiah, the people and God. King Josiah himself read the Conditions of The Covenant that day. King Josiah and the people were one people coming in Covenant with God.

King Josiah and the people came into Covenant with God that the King and the people would walk after The Lord and keep His Commandments. King Josiah even stood on the platform by the pillar during The Blood Covenant Ceremony so all the people could see and hear the Blood Covenant Ceremony taking place. The seriousness of this Promise to God was huge! No one would ever forget the day that they and their King Josiah stood before God and Cut the Blood Covenant publicly. God would not forget, nor would the people, the priests or King Josiah!

After The Blood Covenant Ceremony, King Josiah, along with the people, began doing all that he and the people had come in Covenant to do before God. Much-needed "Housecleaning" began to happen in The Lord's House and in the people because of The Promise or Blood Covenant that had been made that day between King Josiah, the people and God. Truly, Blood Covenant Ceremonies are used throughout the whole Word of God.

Chapter Thirteen

THE ULTIMATE COVENANT CUT

*"And He said to them, This is My blood [which ratifies] the **new covenant**, [the blood] which is being poured out for (on account of) many."* Mark 14:24 (AMP)

*N*ow that we have gone over the ways of the Blood Covenant, we can understand the seriousness, the intensity and commitment of this eternal act. The merging of two families, the Covenant Conditions that the two families will fight others to keep with the other family forever, the selflessness of the Covenant Representatives to cut their own skin and to split open the Covenant Animals and walk through and stand in the midst of the blood. The Covenant Exchange of Names, the Giving of the Coats and Belts represent that each family gives the other their own authority and strength for all situations and the Covenant Meal is shared by all. We have seen how throughout The Bible Blood Covenants were present between God and man and man and man. To what length would God go to show us He is in love with us and that He is serious about us? The answer: He would, even Himself, Cut and be Cut in a Covenant Ceremony.

Remember, "Covenant" in Hebrew is *beriyth (ber-eeth')*, **a compact made by passing between pieces of flesh: covenant, league. To cut, To divide.** The Blood Covenant requires absolute, unwavering loyalty between the two families or people forever. The Blood Covenant mandates that either persons or families would never forget or discontinue their promises and vows to the other for generations. Let's list again the many facets that Cutting a Blood Covenant includes:

Blood Covenant

Representative is Chosen
Covenant Site is Chosen
Conditions of Covenant are decided on and declared
Animal(s) is cut
Walk of Blood
Cutting of Representative's Flesh
Promises Proclaimed and Names are Combined
Giving of Coats
Trading of Belts
Covenant Meal

The Covenant Representative Is Chosen

For many, many years throughout Bible history, it was written about what the Messiah would do, where He would come from, what He would be like and what freedoms He would bring with Him and what we would have as a people who followed Him. Prophets from old spoke and wrote about Him and the benefits The Messiah and His Presence would bring. And even though the Hebrews understood probably more than anyone on this earth the meaning and steps to a Blood Covenant Ceremony, some did not recognize Jesus of Nazareth as the One that would Cut the Ultimate Blood Covenant.

Jesus, The Christ, God's Son, was the One Who was selected to be the Covenant Representative in the New Covenant (or Testament) Ceremony between God and mankind. The first Covenant God made with Adam was broken by Adam. Then God found another man in the earth to Cut a Covenant with and that was Abram, later named Abraham. (We are still attached to the Covenant God made with Adam and Abraham.)

"You are the descendants (sons) of the prophets and the heirs of the covenant which God made and gave to your forefathers, saying to Abraham, And in your Seed (Heir) shall all the families of the earth be blessed and benefited." Acts 3:25 (AMP)

Jesus would represent the Best that Heaven had to offer. He represents to us the best of healing, wholeness, love, joy, peace, prosperity. . . all that God has to offer us if we will come into Covenant with Him. God did not send an angel or some other creation to Cut the Covenant; He sent His only Son, The Firstborn. The One Who is chosen to be the Representative of the Covenant is The One Who carries the *scar* from the Cut during the Blood Covenant Ceremony. Jesus showed the disciples his scars after His Resurrection from the dead:

". . . Jesus came and stood among them and said, "Peace be with you!" 20 After he said this, he showed them his hands and side. The disciples were overjoyed when they saw the Lord." John 20:19-20 (NIV)

"Then he said to Thomas, "Put your finger here; see my hands. Reach out your hand and put it into my side. Stop doubting and believe." John 20:27 (NIV)

The One Who carries the scars of this Blood Covenant is Jesus, The Messiah from Nazareth. He is The Only Representative Who was involved in The Blood Covenant Ceremony on behalf of Father God and Himself. And He has the scars from the Ceremony to prove it! Praise The Lord! And The Bible tells us that He showed others the scars from the Covenant Cut during the Blood Covenant Ceremony. Those scars would always remind Him of His Blood Covenant with us. And to all of those that He showed His scars to after His Resurrection, they told others and those told others and still yet many millions of others, until we have been told of that Blood Covenant Ceremony today and about The One Who carries the scars of it.

The Covenant Sites Were Chosen

When Father God was Cutting a New Blood Covenant with us as His People, He chose His Best to Represent our Big Brother, Jesus. And the Covenant Sites that were chosen by God for Jesus to go to would **pay for the many things that we lost in The Blood Covenant in The Garden of Eden – which was the first Blood Covenant Ceremony of God and Mankind! Mankind didn't carry their side of The Covenant, but God is relentless in carrying His!**

When Adam and Eve lived in the Garden of Eden, it was perfect. It was Heaven on Earth! There was no sickness, disease, curses, lack, unhappiness, worry, shame, fear. . . there was just perfection! Can you imagine, there just wasn't such a thing as a *bad day!* They didn't know what a *headache* or *belly ache was!* Adam and Eve would have no concept of what you would even be saying about things like that! Even the animals all got along with each and with the Man and Woman! There was no danger at all in The Garden! All were protected and provided for. The temperature was always perfect. No storms or coldness–just perfection!

And then when Man and Woman sinned against God and followed the devil and not what God told them to do, sin entered the World through their actions. And when that happened, many consequences for their sin happened, too.

"So the LORD God said to the serpent, "Because you have done this, "Cursed are you above all the livestock and all the wild animals! You will crawl on your belly and

you will eat dust all the days of your life. 15 And I will put enmity between you and the woman, and between your offspring and hers; he will crush your head, and you will strike his heel."

16 To the woman he said, "I will greatly increase your pains in childbearing; with pain you will give birth to children. Your desire will be for your husband, and he will rule over you."

17 To Adam he said, "Because you listened to your wife and ate from the tree about which I commanded you, 'You must not eat of it,' "Cursed is the ground because of you; through painful toil you will eat of it all the days of your life. 18 It will produce thorns and thistles for you, and you will eat the plants of the field. 19 By the sweat of your brow you will eat your food until you return to the ground, since from it you were taken; for dust you are and to dust you will return." Genesis 3:14-19 (NIV)

So, in order for Father God to get back for us all that we lost in The Garden of Eden that day, He made a Way once again, through Blood Covenant through Abraham, Moses, David, Solomon, and the greatest, Jesus!

The Covenant Sites were chosen: The Garden of Gethsemane (which means "oil pressed"), Jerusalem (where His various trials were, the whipping post, and a lot of His beatings and abuse took place here) and at Golgotha, The Place of The Skull, known to many as Calvary. Jesus would begin His Walk of Blood in The Garden of Gethsemane, for Mankind **laid down their Covenant in a Garden (Eden) and that is where Jesus would "pick it up" again, in a Garden!** Blood was shed at these Covenant Sites by the Covenant Representative, Jesus, The Messiah.

At all the Blood Covenant Ceremony Sites, the Other Family that God would be able to come into Covenant with, the other Covenant Family, were present to see The Covenant

Representative for Father God would go through the entire Blood Covenant Ceremony. A few of His disciples saw His Blood Covenant begin in The Garden of Gethsemane, especially Peter, James and John, for He asked them to pray throughout the night and then Jesus would go back and speak to them and ask them why they were asleep. So they saw Him in the first stages of The Blood Covenant Ceremony, where He was sweating *blood.* There were Jesus' family members, some disciples that followed Him throughout the Covenant Sites, the Jewish people of that day, the Jewish Leaders in the various trials, the Romans and all the visitors that had traveled to Jerusalem for the Feast of Passover. So there were Jewish People and Non-Jewish people, Jews and Gentiles, throughout this Blood Covenant Ceremony and all of its Covenant Sites, representing ALL that Jesus bled for in The Blood Covenant!

Some of the people who witnessed the Blood Covenant Ceremony were at all of the Covenant Sites, and yet some only saw part of the Ceremony at one of the Chosen Sites. All of the witnesses present throughout the Cutting of The New Covenant could observe the invitation that was being given by Father God and choose to partake of His benefits that they were watching WITH THEIR VERY EYES!

As King David and King Solomon's Blood Covenant Ceremonies were Ceremonies that had many Covenant Sites, so too would be the case in Father God's New Blood Covenant that He was Cutting with Man. The Garden of Gethsemane, throughout The City of Jerusalem, and Golgotha were the Sites at this Blood Covenant. And just like King David and King Solomon's Blood Covenant Ceremonies, all Three Kings (David, Solomon and Jesus) would walk themselves in *blood!* And just like David and Solomon's Blood Covenant Ceremonies, all *were mobile, and Jesus would be mobile, too–very mobile!*

Covenant Conditions &
Promises Proclaimed

The Covenant Condition and The Promises Proclaimed were discussed and declared for thousands of years by God's prophets and people as they told all who would listen that when The Messiah would arrive that He would be a part of a Blood Covenant Ceremony and would pay for many benefits for His people and for the people themselves. Examples of the Conditions that were spoken about Jesus and The Blood Covenant He would do and The Conditions that Jesus would come into Covenant with His people are:

"But He was wounded for our transgressions, He was bruised for our iniquities; The chastisement for our peace was upon Him, And by His stripes we are healed." Isaiah 53:5 (NKJV)

". . . for He [God] Himself has said, I will not in any way fail you nor give you up nor leave you without support. [I WILL] NOT, [I WILL] NOT, [I WILL] NOT in any degree leave you helpless nor forsake nor let [you] down (relax My hold on you)! [Assuredly not!]" Deuteronomy 31:6, Hebrews 13:5 (AMP)

". . . Cursed is every one that hangeth on a tree:" Deuteronomy 21:23, Galatians 3:13 (KJV)

The Messiah would also be for us all in battle, *"Who is this King of glory? The LORD strong and mighty, the LORD mighty in battle."* Psalm 24:8 (AMP)

The Covenant Conditions and Promises that were paid for by The Covenant Representative, Jesus, were massive. As stated earlier, throughout The Old Covenant (which means "Testament"), many told what The Messiah would bring and pay for within what we now can see was a Blood Covenant

Ceremony. And yet, all of The Blood Covenant Conditions and Promises that we see throughout The Word that came from previous Blood Covenants were also included. Those Blood Covenant Conditions and Promises from Abraham, Moses, David and Solomon and now Jesus, were all *absorbed* into The New Blood Covenant! Jesus built on top of those Blood Covenants and extended those foundational Promises, and He made them better for those who would come into Covenant with Him! He made it all better and bigger for His Covenant Family! Jesus didn't invalidate and cancel out what God had already come into Blood Covenant with His People about; no, Jesus built right on top of them and made them all better!

All of what I like to call *the hard things* that were in the Older Blood Covenants, Jesus accomplished by using *Himself,* so that *those hard things* would be enhanced and achieved. For example, one of the Covenant Conditions that was given to Moses and the Hebrew Children was that they were to kill a lamb at The Feast of Passover. Well, now we don't have to sacrifice a lamb or any animal, because Jesus took that *hard thing* and paid for it Himself.

> *"Do not think that I have come to do away with or undo the Law or the Prophets; I have come not to do away with or undo but to complete and fulfill them."* Matthew 5:17 (AMP)

> *"Then He said to them, This is what I told you while I was still with you: everything which is written con-cerning Me in the <u>Law of Moses</u> and the <u>Prophets</u> and the <u>Psalms</u> must be fulfilled."* Luke 24:44 (AMP)

What Jesus paid for DID NOT CANCEL that Covenant Condition; it is still inside that Blood Covenant that was made. He just made the Way so that it was taken care of *forever through Himself!* He made the New Blood Covenant so, so, so much bigger for us! God had a Blood Covenant with Abraham, Moses, David and Solomon and with each Covenant

Ceremony more and more Conditions and Promises were built on! So when God sent His Representative for The New Blood Covenant Ceremony, he built *everything* into it!

Now, what is so great about what Jesus did is that He not only took *everything* from The Blood Covenant Ceremonies with Abraham, Moses, David and Solomon, He also took all that was written and spoken about Him by The Prophets and in The Psalms—He took it all and **put it ALL in The New Blood Covenant!** So we can have ALL that was Promised!

And it doesn't stop there! Then Jesus, as The Blood Covenant Representative, *says even more things that He will do, Father God will do, what The Holy Spirit will do, what we are entitled to have. . . AND SO MUCH MORE!* **The Covenant Conditions and The Promises Proclaimed kept coming and coming and still yet, coming!** The Covenant Conditions and The Promises Proclaimed kept coming through Jesus throughout the first part of The New Testament (which means "Covenant") of your Bibles!

Jesus kept speaking The Conditions of Covenant and kept building on top of what we already have through the Older Covenants! Our New Blood Covenant is so LARGE that Jesus continually kept adding Promises and Covenant Conditions for approximately 3 1/2 years, while He was doing His Ministry! He kept speaking Those Covenant Conditions right up to The Covenant Meal. The final Covenant Conditions that Jesus spoke we could have if we would be in Covenant with Him were at The Covenant Meal he had with His disciples. They were Luke 22:26-30, 35-38 and John 13:3-20, 31-35 and John Chapters 14, 15, 16, 17. **And when He gave His last Covenant Conditions at this Covenant Meal, the Conditions were complete. Covenant Promises and Conditions are not spoken of past this point. Action to purchase the Conditions begins.**

Jesus has met and is still meeting all the Conditions of the Covenant that have been made. He'll never forget them and He wrote them down *so we wouldn't either!*

The Covenant Meal

Jesus, The Covenant Representative, spoke what Father God told Him to speak. What Father God wanted to add to The Blood Covenant Conditions, He had His Representative do again throughout Jesus' Ministry, right up to and within The Covenant Meal.

The Covenant Meal is normally done at the end of a Blood Covenant Ceremony, but Father God decided it to be at the beginning of this New Covenant. And what we must see is that The Covenant Meal will BEGIN The Blood Covenant Ceremony! The Covenant Meal that Jesus had with His disciples the night of His betrayal was that of the Passover Meal. The Covenant Meals that would take place in other Blood Covenants in history included bread and wine, also. Let's look again at what would transpire in Ancient Blood Covenant Ceremonies that we read about earlier.

The Covenant Meal is normally the last part of the Blood Covenant Ceremony. The two Representatives of the families coming into Covenant, the leaders and all the family members have a Covenant Meal together. The most important items of this Covenant Meal are the *bread and the wine.* When the bread is eaten by the two Covenant Families it represents to each other as if to say:

"Now that we are in Blood Covenant with each other,
I would eat my own flesh *before I would let you die! You will never be alone again!"*

And when the wine is drunk by the two Covenant families during The Blood Covenant Ceremony, it is representing to the other family that:

"This wine is like the blood of my body. My blood is my life. As we drink this wine together, my life is now your life."

164

Is this beginning to sound like the language that Jesus was saying at His Covenant Meal? Jesus knew the "ways" of The Blood Covenant Ceremony and *He was fulfilling them all!* Even to the point of saying out loud, as The Covenant Representative:

"Now as they were eating, Jesus took bread and, praising God, gave thanks and asked Him to bless it to their use, and when He had broken it, He gave it to the disciples and said, **Take, eat; this is My body.** *27 And He took a cup, and when He had given thanks, He gave it to them, saying, Drink of it, all of you;* **28 For this is My blood of the <u>new</u> <u>covenant</u>,** *which [ratifies the agreement and] is being poured out for many for the forgiveness of sins."* Matthew 26:26-28 (AMP)

Wow! He was speaking Blood Covenant Talk from the Blood Covenant Ceremony from the past now, fulfilling one in the present and for our future! He was saying what had been said for thousands of years during this Blood Covenant Ceremony at the time of the Covenant Meal.

And that is, that as you eat this bread, it's as if it is My Body! And as you drink this wine, it is as if it is my very own blood. But since we are now in a <u>New</u> Covenant with Jesus, He tells us that when we eat of bread and drink of some grape juice (fruit of the vine) **it IS His Body and it IS His Blood!** No more Blood Covenant Ceremonies will ever be needed again! For Jesus, The Firstborn and Covenant Representative fulfilled what was required to merge two families together and all their strengths together forever. . . and that was ONLY by fulfilling The Blood Covenant Ceremony.

<u>Remember</u>

". . . On the night when he was betrayed, the Lord Jesus took some bread 24 and gave thanks to God for

*it. Then he broke it in pieces and said, "This is my body, which is given for you. **Do this to remember me."** 25 In the same way, he took the cup of wine after supper, saying, **"This cup is the new covenant between God and his people—an agreement confirmed with my blood. Do this to remember me** as often as you drink it."* 1Corinthians 11:23-25 (NLT)

In the Ancient Blood Covenant Ceremonies, the families that had been joined always partook of the bread and wine in The Covenant Meal. It was to signify that even if their own bodies and their own blood would have to be given for the other, it would be. And the Covenant Meal was to **remind** all of the members of the two families and the generations to come in the two families that they were now in Covenant and if need be, they were to sacrifice their own bodies and blood for the other. And what did Jesus tell His disciples that night, the night of His betrayal, that is so significant here? He said:

"This cup is the new covenant between God and his people—an agreement confirmed with my blood. Do this to remember me. . ."

He was clearly stating that He was representing God and the disciples were representing "His People!" And a New Covenant in BLOOD was about to happen, and it would be done by God's Representative, Jesus, The Firstborn of God - God's Best to Represent Him and His Kingdom in The Blood Covenant Ceremony! *(Remember, it was protocol for the two families that were to enter into Covenant with one another to pick the representative that would be the best they had to offer. In Father God's case, His Best was Jesus!)*

And what was the additional message that Jesus communicated at the Covenant Meal that we call the Passover Meal?

Do this to remember Me! Do this to remember the New Blood Covenant that we have with each other now.

Do this (take of the bread and the fruit of the vine. . . My Body and My Blood) to remind you of the New Covenant Conditions that I have made with you. . . you as the other family Father God is now in Covenant with. Do this to remember of this time that I, as God's Representative, was The Covenant Animal that took The Covenant Cuts on My Body!

When you do this, remember later on tonight and all day tomorrow and all that I will do for you in this Blood Covenant Ceremony for the next 24 hours! Remember it for yourself and remember it to tell others and bring them in to this Covenant with Father God!

Now, as we stated earlier, The Covenant Meal that was within The Blood Covenant Ceremony that Jesus fulfilled was during the Passover Meal. We have to remember that Jesus partook of The Covenant Meal with His disciples on the same night that His Blood Covenant Ceremony began.

Jesus and His disciples went from "the Upper Room" where they took the Passover Meal, which was also The Covenant Meal of the Blood Covenant Ceremony. (The disciples just didn't know that The Covenant <u>had</u> <u>begun</u> <u>with</u> <u>The</u> <u>Covenant</u> <u>Meal</u>.) The Covenant didn't begin the next day. The Covenant began the very night that He fulfilled the Covenant Meal element *". . . on the night He was betrayed."* 1 Corinthians 11:23 (NIV)

And we know that Judas Iscariot betrayed Jesus in The Garden of Gethsemane, which is on The Mount of Olives. *(The Betrayal of Judas happened in The Garden, just as God's betrayal happened in A Garden! The Covenant Representative, Jesus, was making <u>everything</u> right in this Blood Covenant Ceremony!)* In that Garden is where Jesus' Blood was first shed. And that was the first Covenant Site where Blood flowed and the Walk of Blood began for Him.

In addition to this Covenant Meal that Jesus partook of, we also know that He has stated to us at that meal:

"I tell you the truth, I will not drink again of the fruit of the vine until that day when I drink it anew in the kingdom of God." Mark 14:25 (NIV)

Jesus will also have another Special and Exclusive Meal with His Church, and that will be at the Marriage Supper of The Lamb (Revelation 19:9)! At both of these Extraordinary Meals, the Blood Covenant Meal of old and The Marriage Supper of The Lamb will have something in common, and that is that the two "families" that have merged together are present at both Meals.

We see the two "families" that have joined – Jesus, The Bridegroom, The Blood Covenant Ceremony Representative of Heaven. . . and us, The People who for thousands of years have received the invitation to enter into Covenant and receive all of the benefits purchased for us, now His Family - His Bride.

And we will be able to attend this Family Meal called the Wedding Supper of The Lamb (The Covenant Animal That Was Cut), for we decided to merge ourselves with The Blood Covenant Representative, Jesus, and His Family with Father God. We decided to receive ALL of The Blood Covenant Ceremony that Father God provided for us through His Representative, Jesus. And this very special Meal that we will be able to attend in our future was bought and paid for with The Blood Covenant Ceremony that happened a long time ago.

The Giving of The Coat

The Giving of the Coat, which represents the giving of a person's authority, was done by Jesus, God's Representative, with the other representatives (the disciples –representing us) in this amazing Covenant. We find Jesus at the Covenant Meal or The Passover Meal that He shared with His disciples on the same night that He went to Gethsemane, the Garden where He sweat great drops of blood in making His decision to go to the Cross. This same night, prior to going to Gethsemane,

He told His disciples to prepare for the Passover Meal (see Matthew 26:17-19),

At this Meal, we find the Blood Covenant Ceremony, also. Jesus, knowing that the time had come for Him and the Covenant Ceremony to begin, decided at that moment to Give His Coat or Robe, the symbol of His Authority to those in the room.

> *"So he got up from the table, **took off his robe,. . .** wrapped a towel around his waist, 5 and poured water into a basin. Then he began to wash the disciples' feet, drying them with the towel he had around him."* John 13:4-5 (NLT)

Jesus not only conferred and gave over His Authority at this point as God's Representative by laying down His Coat or Robe for others, He did so throughout other Covenant Ceremony Sites He went to. He was getting back the authority that was lost by Adam. The Blood of God's Representative at this beginning of the Covenant, which was at the Covenant Meal, was also present. Jesus told His disciples to begin at this point to drink His Blood and eat His Body.

> *"Now as they were eating, Jesus took bread and, praising God, gave thanks and asked Him to bless it to their use, and when He had broken it, He gave it to the disciples and said, **Take, eat; this is My body.** 27 And He took a cup, and when He had given thanks, He gave it to them, saying, Drink of it, all of you; **28 For this is My blood of the new covenant,** which [ratifies the agreement and] is being poured out for many for the forgiveness of sins."* Matthew 26:26-28 (AMP)

The Blood Covenant Ceremony had begun! And this time it began within The Covenant Meal. One of God's rules is the last will be first and the first last, as it was in the Covenant Meal in The New Blood Covenant.

Fair Trade?

As we have stated in the earlier sections of this book, the Giving of the Coats element of The Blood Covenant Ceremony is when the two representatives take off their coats and give them to the other representative. *And this is done in blood of The Covenant Animal.*

The coat signifies authority. For example, a military coat represents the authority and rank of a person. When the coats are exchanged the two representatives are saying on behalf of themselves and their families who are all present and witnessing,

> *All that I am and who I am, I give to you. I give you all my authority. You may use my authority to live your life. You have my authority now and I have yours.*

As is customary with The Blood Covenant Ceremony, **both** sides of the "families" give over their coats or robes to signify the giving of their authority and power. We see the ones who would be partaking of The Ceremony that day that represented you and me as Gentiles and that would be the Roman soldiers. Matthew 27:28,31 (AMP) tells us:

> *"And they stripped off His clothes and **put a scarlet robe (garment of dignity and office worn by Roman officers of rank) upon Him,**. . . 31 And when they finished making sport of Him, **they stripped Him of the robe** and **put His own garments on Him** and led Him away to be crucified."*

The Giving of The Coat or Robe in The Blood Covenant Ceremony to Jesus was done by our representatives (the Romans) as a mockery to God and His Representative, Jesus, during The Ceremony! The representatives (the Roman soldiers) took a Robe or Coat that an "officer of rank" had worn and gave it or placed it on Jesus.

The Coat or Robe the Roman soldiers gave on our behalf to God and Jesus represented fear, shame, ignorance of Truth, anger, enslavement to a government, theft, great captivity and sin. We had no true authority to give that day that anyone would really want. Yet God loved us enough to take <u>our</u> offer **and wear the robe that represented us, the scarlet robe**!

As for the Coat or Robe we gave in The Blood Covenant Ceremony, we even stole it back from The Representative of God, stripping it off of Him and leaving The Coat or Robe with blood stains from God's Representative, Jesus! The Coats were "traded" in Blood, but it was all Jesus' Blood in the Trading of Coats in this Ceremony!

Both Family Representatives in The Giving of The Coat part of the Blood Covenant Ceremony had blood on them and on their Robes or Coats. Jesus did so by bleeding on the Robe that the Roman Soldiers put on Him and then took off. And Jesus' Robe that the Soldiers took off of Him had His Blood on it, also.

Jesus' Blood would be on Himself and the Soldiers, too, by carrying the Robe or Coat of God's Representative. Therefore, The Giving of The Coats/ Robes, which is Giving of your Authority, was fulfilled in Blood, just as it always has in The Blood Covenant Ceremony! How unselfish it is that God still wanted to be in Covenant with us! He traded Coats and Authority with us – *amazing!*

The Trading of The Belt

The Trading of The Belts in the Blood Covenant Ceremony, which represents all the weaponry one gives to another, was also executed by Jesus. In John 13:4 (NLT) we also see Jesus having His Belt on His waist, **a towel,** representing His Authority as a Servant, *"So he got up from the table, took off his robe,* **wrapped a towel around his waist,. . ."**

We later see Jesus taking off His Belt and submitting it to the other Representatives in The Ceremony, His disciples. Yet God's Representative in this Blood Covenant Ceremony is taking off His Belt (His Towel), transferring it to the other People that He is coming in Covenant with and SHOWING THEM HOW TO USE THE AUTHORITY THAT IS BEING GIVEN THEM!

> *"When he had finished washing their feet, he put on his clothes and returned to his place. "Do you understand what I have done for you?" he asked them. 13 "You call me 'Teacher' and 'Lord,' and rightly so, for that is what I am. 14 Now that I, your Lord and Teacher, have washed your feet, you also should wash one another's feet. 15 I have set you an example that you should do as I have done for you. 16 I tell you the truth, no servant is greater than his master, nor is a messenger greater than the one who sent him. 17 Now that you know these things, you will be blessed if you do them." John 13:12-17 (NIV)*

Jesus' Belt was a Towel that He used to hand over and display His Authority to the disciples then and to us now. Throughout The Covenant Ceremony, Jesus shows us that when we receive Jesus', The Representative's, Authority, is most powerful when we are serving and "washing" others of their dirt they get from sin and the World. How marvelous that The King of Heaven and Earth would choose a Towel for His Belt in The Blood Covenant Ceremony to hand over His Weaponry! Jesus, God's Representative, would exemplify through the Ceremony that REAL AUTHORITY is present and administered when one serves!

More Arsenal We Received

We can find in Ephesians 6:10-18 an assortment of the arsenal that Jesus recovered and has given to us to use in the battles we face here on earth:

"Finally, be strong in the Lord and in his mighty power. *11 Put on **the full armor of God** so that you can take your stand against the devil's schemes. 12 For our struggle is not against flesh and blood, but against the rulers, against the authorities, against the powers of this dark world and against the spiritual forces of evil in the heavenly realms. 13 Therefore put on the full armor of God, so that when the day of evil comes, you may be able to stand your ground, and after you have done everything, to stand.*

*14 Stand firm then, with **the belt** of truth buckled around your waist, with **the breastplate** of righteousness in place, 15 and with your feet fitted with the readiness that comes from the gospel of peace. 16 In addition to all this, take up **the shield** of faith, with which you can extinguish all the flaming arrows of the evil one. 17 Take **the helmet** of salvation and **the sword** of the Spirit, which is the word of God. 18 And **pray in the Spirit** on all occasions with all kinds of prayers and requests. With this in mind, be alert and always keep on praying for all the saints."*

In the Trading of the Belts part of The Blood Covenant Ceremony, as we can recall from previous writing, the belts of weapons are taken off. In this case it is Jesus' towel from His waist. This exchange represents that:

I give you all my strength. Your enemies are now mine. I'll fight for you even if I die. When you go to battle I will always be by your side, fighting with you and for you and your family, even to the death. I shall serve you even unto death.

All of the weaponry that Jesus died and bled to give us is more than enough to fight our enemy and His. The artillery and strength that was forfeited by Adam was purchased back through the actions and death of God's Representative, Jesus, The Christ of Nazareth, The Last Adam! So when we need to fight and cast our enemy, the devil and his cohorts out of our "gardens", all of the weaponry needed to do so is now in our possession. And it was all bought back for us throughout The Blood Covenant Ceremony!

Chapter Fourteen

THE COVENANT ANIMAL
& THE WALK OF BLOOD

The Covenant Animal that would be selected for the Covenant Ceremony, as we have seen, was usually a heifer, ram, goat or the other named animals in The Bible. And it was the best the Covenant Families had to offer. The Covenant Animal for this New Blood Covenant was from Heaven and was selected by Father God, and it was Jesus, The Lamb of God. This Lamb was and is The Best and He is without a spot or blemish. . . The Perfect Sacrifice and Covenant Animal! God gave His Very Best!

Jesus, Heaven's Covenant Animal, was beaten, chained, bruised, flogged, crucified and pierced. Jesus, The Covenant Animal, was Cut repeatedly in MANY WAYS on His body, bringing forth blood in many ways and places. The Covenant Animal would continually move in Blood!

The Garden

He began The Covenant Blood part of this Covenant Ceremony in The Garden of Gethsemane. The Bible says that He sweated great drops of *blood.*

"And being in an agony he prayed more earnestly: and his sweat was as it were great drops of blood falling down to the ground." Luke 22:44 (KJV)

And yet we know that Covenant Conditions were stated many years later that The Messiah and Covenant Representative would be in great agony. In Matthew 26:38 Jesus says in the Garden, *"Then he said to them, "My soul is overwhelmed <u>with sorrow</u> to the point of death. . . ."* And then we see The Bible tell us that a Covenant Condition that would be fulfilled in the New Blood Covenant is:

*"Surely he hath borne our griefs, and carried our **<u>sorrows</u>**:"* Isaiah 53:4(KJV)

Jesus was doing something here, wasn't He? He was accomplishing just one of MANY Covenant Conditions and Promises that would be within this Blood Covenant Ceremony. And *blood* had to be shed right here, right in the Garden, because we lost SO MUCH in the Garden of Eden. Only Blood in The Blood Covenant Ceremony at this Covenant Site would get us back all that we lost! Let's look again at what resulted in the sin that Man and Woman started.

"So the Lord *God said to the serpent, "Because you have done this, "Cursed are you above all the livestock and all the wild animals! You will <u>put enmity between you and the woman, and between your offspring and hers; he will crush your head, and you will strike his heel</u>."*

16 To the woman he said, "I will greatly increase your pains in childbearing; with pain you will give birth to children. Your desire will be for your husband, and he will rule over you."

17 To Adam he said, "Because you listened to your wife and ate from the tree about which I commanded you,

'You must not eat of it,' "Cursed is the ground because of you; through painful toil you will eat of it all the days of your life. 18 It will produce thorns and thistles for you, and you will eat the plants of the field. 19 By the sweat of your brow you will eat your food until you return to the ground, since from it you were taken; for dust you are and to dust you will return." Genesis 3:14-19 (NIV)

Of course, we know that verse 15 above is specifically talking about Jesus, The Covenant Representative, Who will be The One Who will crush the devil's head (his authority) with His heel. Jesus would shed blood through His very own pores in The Garden of Gethsemane and begin the sacrifice of His Blood to take away all of the authority that the devil obtained in The Garden of Eden.

In verse 16 he was releasing women from bondage. In Galatians 3:28 (NLT) it tells us, *"There is no longer Jew or Gentile, slave or free, male and female. For you are all one in Christ Jesus."* What the woman (Man with a womb) lost in The Garden, Jesus was getting back for her! She would now be one in Christ Jesus! There were no more dividers of who a woman (Man with a womb) was. Man and Woman were created in God's image. She was created to be like the Man and to not be "ruled" over. As we can see in The Old Testament, women were sometimes not treated correctly. Jesus brought us as women back to our original place, as it was in The Garden. We are still to be under the "covering" and "authority" of our husbands. But that is a freedom, not a "rulership."

In verse 17, we see that *even the ground was cursed!* But of course, our Blood Covenant Representative took the care from that! His Blood fell on that ground in that Garden and took away that curse! Following the plan of God and even dealing with your finances will take the "toil" away from you! Dewayne and I *finally* began to listen to God and follow His leading in our finances, and we have been debt free for many years now. And our Ministry, *Jamie Carte Ministries* is debt free also and always has been. The "toil" that debt had on us personally was huge. We got over into God's Way of doing finances and it has brought us "ease" not "toil." So Jesus has made a way for you and all that will follow to remove the "toil" from your life.

In verse 18 we can see that the curse is covering mankind's Harvest. Your Harvest under the curse would just produce thorns and thistles. *And that is why Jesus Christ wore a **crown of thorns!*** The abusive action and mockery that He underwent by wearing that crown of thorns was to revoke the curse of a dry and parched Land and Harvest for you and me! When we plant "seeds" in The Kingdom of God, we can expect goodness and blessings and Harvest to come back to us. . . not thorns! The King wore a crown of thorns to give His Authority over the curse that was given in the Garden of Eden and give His Covenant Family back their inheritance and their Harvest! And **blood** came from His Head with those thorns on it! We again rule the Ground and the Land, Man and Woman of God! And it's because our Blood Covenant Representative, Jesus, paid for that right by wearing those "thorns" on His Head and blood coming from them!

In verse 19 we see from the curse given because mankind sinned that we would have to sweat or worry or fret or be anxious in this life for what we need. Sweat from our brows, which is where you think from, isn't it? The worrying and concern that comes from life does not have to be for a person in Blood Covenant with Jesus, for *blood was shed from the agony that Jesus carried in the Garden!*

"And being in an agony he prayed more earnestly: and his sweat was as it were great drops of blood falling down to the ground." Luke 22:44 (KJV)

No more Child of God in Covenant! God's Covenant Representative took it all and sweated blood over it for you! He covered you in blood in The Garden, so that you would not have to live under the curse of what we lost in The Garden of Eden! Blood was being shed for you and me as The Blood Covenant Representative was moving from one Covenant Site to the next. And *this* Blood Covenant was enveloping what happened in the first Garden, where the **First Blood Covenant Began!**

Covenant Site, Jerusalem

We know that blood is essential to fulfill Covenant. And we see that when Jesus is arrested in The Garden, that is where *our freedom began.* Jesus sweated great drops of blood from the "pressure" that He was experiencing and when they came to Jesus in The Garden, He still had that blood on Him. Heaven's Covenant Animal was beaten, chained, bruised and whipped, bringing forth blood throughout several hours from His time in the Garden to the Cross.

He is walking and being beaten and mistreated in His journey to Jerusalem and also when He is in The City–by many men, not just a few. The Bible tells us that a "Company" of soldiers mistreated Jesus. A Company of soldiers was a division in the Roman legion that was approximately 200 men! That would be in addition to all the others that The Bible speaks of that mistreated and abused Jesus.

"Then the governor's soldiers took Jesus into the Praetorium and gathered the whole <u>company</u> of soldiers around him. 28 They <u>stripped him</u> and put a scarlet robe on him, 29 and then twisted together a <u>crown of thorns</u> and set it on his head. They put a staff in his right hand and knelt in front of him and <u>mocked him.</u> "Hail, king of the Jews!" they said. 30 They <u>spit on him,</u> and took the staff and <u>struck him on the head again and again.</u>" Matthew 27:27-30 (NIV)

"So Judas, obtaining and taking charge of the band of soldiers and some guards (attendants) of the high priests and Pharisees, came there with lanterns and torches and <u>weapons.</u>" John 18:3 (AMP)

He is beaten during His trials and His beard is pulled out. Again, bringing forth *blood out of The Covenant Animal.*

"When Jesus said this, one of the officials nearby struck him in the face. "Is this the way you answer the high priest?" he demanded. 23 "If I said something wrong," Jesus replied, "testify as to what is wrong. But if I spoke the truth, why did you strike me?" 24 Then Annas sent him, still bound, to Caiaphas the high priest." (John 18:22-24 (NIV))

"Then they <u>spat in His face</u> and <u>struck Him with their fists</u>; and some <u>slapped Him in the face</u>," Matthew 26:67 (AMP)

"The men who were guarding Jesus began mocking and <u>beating him</u>." (Luke 22:63 (NIV))

"I gave my back to the smiters, and my <u>cheeks to them that plucked off the hair</u>: I hid not my face from shame and spitting." Isaiah 50:6 (KJV)

<u>It's Hard To Conceive</u>

Jesus, The Covenant Animal, was Cut in MANY WAYS in His body repeatedly, bringing forth blood in many ways and places. From all the "Legal Trials" that Our Covenant Representative had to attend, He then chooses to submit to being flogged.

"So then Pilate took Jesus and scourged (flogged, whipped) Him." John 19:1 (AMP)

I know for years when I read that Jesus was flogged, I really didn't know what that would entail. But after research and, like many of you, seeing *The Passion of The Christ* movie, I understand. The Bible states that *flogging* happens to Him in a sentence. So much happened within that one sentence! But what flogging did to a person was horrendous! Flogging killed most people! Jesus could have "given up The Ghost" as He said He did on the Cross, but He kept going through all that He did, so that He would **complete the Blood Covenant Ceremony!**

Blood coming from His pores, from His brow from the crown of thorns, from His face from the beatings and His hair being plucked out of His beard. *Blood is streaming down Him* from being struck on the head and from other parts of His Body from the beatings. His flesh is hanging off of His back, the back of His legs and His sides and blood is pouring down His Body from the flogging. **The Bible says that you could not even recognize Him to be a human!**

"Many who were appalled at him—his appearance was so disfigured beyond that of any man and his form marred beyond human likeness" Isaiah 52:14 (NIV)

Our Covenant Representative was beaten to the point that The Bible says He was disfigured! That He didn't look like He was human! *Can we grasp that?* Jesus is allowing *the very ones that this is for,* representing you and me, to make Him look like He isn't even a human! Could it be that because of the beatings and floggings that He looked more like an animal than human? Our precious Savior and Friend was giving of everything that He had for us! He was bringing *so much freedom* to us! I'm sure He kept telling Himself:

I can't quit, I have to make the Walk of Blood all the way, not quit here at the whipping post! I'm broken inside. Their words have crushed me. Their fists have bruised me. My flesh on my back and body is just hanging from me and my body is literally been split open. It's getting so hard to move. I taste the sweat and blood streaming down my face. It's flowing into my eyes. I'm exhausted. And yet I must move forward.

I've fallen. I must get back up. I'm not finished yet. I will not stop this. I love them so much. Father, I will finish this Blood Covenant!

The Covenant Representative, The Covenant Animal, The Covenant Blood – All in One, IN JESUS! The Blood Covenant was moving in Jerusalem AGAIN! The Ark of The Covenant was in The Temple, but God wanted His Presence to not be in ONE PLACE at ONE TIME, SO THE BLOOD COVENANT WAS MOVING IN JERUSALEM TO MOVE HIM, GOD! Jesus was building on ALL THOSE FORMER COVENANTS AND MAKING THEM BETTER AND NEW!

Jesus is completely **COVERED in Blood!** The Covenant Animal is CUT and Blood is drenching Him and the streets of Jerusalem. And everyone that is around Him or even beating Him, whipping Him and flogging Him has GOT HIS BLOOD ON THEM, TOO! **And what is He doing? He's walking from one Covenant Site to the other! Fulfilling The Walk of Blood!** *The Covenant Animal **kept walking** while being sacrificed!*

Jesus was The Covenant Representative AND The Covenant Animal and The Blood! This Covenant Animal was Cut, and yet this Covenant Animal is Walking *in His Own Blood.* This Covenant Animal was not Cut just once. He is Cut over and over and over. Many Covenant Animals were Cut in King David and King Solomon's Blood Covenant Ceremonies. **Only One Covenant Animal is in this Ceremony, yet Cut Many Times!**

The Cut at Calvary

The Covenant Representative is Cut in His Flesh. This element of the Blood Covenant Ceremony requires the Chosen Covenant Representatives to be cut on their wrists and blood to flow. Both of Jesus' wrists were "cut" by the nails stabbing through His Flesh, where once again His Blood flowed. Also, nails were pounded into His feet so that He would hang up in the air, for all to see.

> ". . . Cursed is every one that hangeth on a tree:" Deuteronomy 21:23, Galatians 3:13 (KJV)

His Blood was also flowing out of His feet. So not only did He fulfill the Blood Covenant Ceremony by His hands or wrists being cut and bleeding, Jesus had blood coming out of His feet, **symbolizing the Covenant Representative having blood at his feet and around His ankles while in the Covenant Animal's blood! Jesus was the Blood Covenant Representative and The Covenant Animal that was Cut, and He had His Own Blood on His Own Feet - God fulfilling _every_ detail!**

Why were there two other individuals that day going to hang on crosses? For, we know that there was a hurry to not have bodies hanging on the crosses due to the Feast of Passover taking place. That is why the soldiers broke the legs of the two other men on the crosses that day with Jesus. They were trying to hurry their dying process. So, why two other men, why not just one other man? Why was Jesus in the center of the two men? Why did the soldiers place Him in the center and not on one of the outer ends? Because The Covenant Representative had to be in between two pieces of flesh! Now, we know that The Covenant Animals are Cut in The Blood Covenant Ceremony into halves and are placed to face each other, so that in the center of the two halves of flesh is the flow of blood. When The Covenant Animal, Jesus, hung on the cross He hung **between two thieves, two men, TWO PIECES OF FLESH!**

His blood flowing out of Him was in the center of the two pieces of flesh (the two men)! He was not only the Covenant Animal, He was also the Covenant Blood that was between the two parts of flesh (men opposite of Jesus on the Cross), so that The Blood flowed into

the center in accordance with the protocol of The Blood Covenant Ceremony! The Blood Himself flowed between the Two Pieces of Flesh that day!

Distant Shores Media/Sweet Publishing

The Last Cut

There were SO MANY COVENANT CUTS that were made on Jesus. And then we find one more Cut that happened on The Covenant Animal.

"But one of the soldiers pierced <u>His side</u> with a spear, and immediately <u>blood</u> and <u>water</u> came (flowed) out." John 19:34 (AMP)

And as we covered earlier, out of that Last Covenant Cut flowed blood and water and birthed Jesus' Bride, The Church! God used an "incision" on the First Adam's side to deliver his bride, "Woman." And out of The Last Adam's Side, the blood and water in Him came out by the spear to His Side to birth His Bride, The Church! The Bride was born out of Jesus' Blood and Water. We are born once in the Natural and then we are to be Born Again through Jesus! That Last Covenant Cut allowed all that was left inside The Covenant Animal and Representative to come gushing out! Jesus said, *"It is Finished!"* and then gave up His Spirit. He had excellently accomplished The Blood Covenant Ceremony in its entirety.

And yet even after Jesus had given up His Spirit, He continued to build onto our Covenant with Him. He defeated Death, Hell and The Grave!

"O death, where is thy sting? O grave, where is thy victory?" 1Cor.15:55 (KJV)

"For Christ died for sins once for all, the righteous for the unrighteous, to bring you to God. **He was put to death in the body** but made **alive by the Spirit,** 19 **through whom also he went and preached to the spirits in prison. . ."** 1 Peter 3:18-19 (NIV)

Jesus tasted death so we wouldn't have to! He went to the grave and experienced the grave so we wouldn't have to!

He conquered Hell and took all of the keys from it! *Can you imagine how angry that makes the Devil–to not even have keys to your own place!* Then Jesus took His Blood as The Blood Covenant Representative and High Priest with The Covenant Animal's Blood (His Own) and went and put it in Heaven's Tabernacle in The Holy of Holies!

> *"When Christ came as high priest of the good things that are already here, <u>he went through the greater and more perfect tabernacle that is not man-made</u>, that is to say, not a part of this creation. 12 He did not enter by means of the blood of goats and calves; but **he entered the Most Holy Place once for all by his own blood,** having obtained eternal redemption."* Hebrews 9:11-12 (NIV)

Why did Jesus do so much? Because He loves us. Because He was and is obedient to The Father and because He was fulfilling ALL OF The Blood Covenant. **For The Covenant Animal had to die. . .** *so He did!* And He had to finish and get back what we lost in The Garden of Eden.

Names Combined

Also, the two thieves that hung on both sides of Jesus that day demonstrated the Covenant Promises to be accomplished. One thief received Jesus Christ as his Lord; the Bible gives us no record that the other did. Jesus was the Covenant Representative that day for Father God and His Kingdom. One thief united himself with Father God's Family being represented there that day. He decided to accept the offer that this Blood Covenant Ceremony, the Kingdom of God and Father God were offering. He decided to become a part of the Family Jesus was representing. The other thief decided to stay with the offer that he had with the Kingdom of Darkness and with the devil. This was a picture of what millions would do from this day forward in history to accept God's Covenant Promises, paid for or not.

Next, the Covenant Promises and prophecies that had been proclaimed about the Messiah or the New Covenant Representative were now being displayed before everyone's eyes! And all while the Representative and Covenant Animal, Jesus, is bleeding and fulfilling the Promises before them!

On that day and every day since then, anyone who would give their lives to Jesus and live for Him would now receive the Covenant Promises that He paid for and displayed on that day.

If you accept the Conditions of The Blood Covenant that Jesus fulfilled, you can be grafted into The Family of God! See, the ONLY way you can become a part of This Family, *is you must come by blood and be born again.* You were born into the family line of Adam when you were birthed in the Earth. And therefore you and I came under the "Curse" that resulted after Man and Woman sinned. But God has been making a way and making a way and still making a way for you and me throughout history through all The Blood Covenants He's made, moving Mankind forward to get us back into right standing with Him and to possess all that we started out with in The Garden of Eden and *even more,* until finally we arrive at The New Blood Covenant that Jesus so wonderfully accomplished! *Thank You, Lord!*

All these years later, an invitation to come into The Family is still available through Blood Covenant. Even though you were not in Jerusalem that day watching all of The Blood Covenant Ceremony take place when Jesus was fulfilling it throughout the Garden of Gethsemane, on all the streets of Jerusalem and then on to Calvary, you can still join The Family of God. You must believe and receive what the Family of God's Representative, Jesus, did throughout The Blood Covenant Ceremony to make for us the New Testament (New Covenant). That's what is so fantastic about Covenant: Generations and generations to come can be a part of The Conditions of Covenant and be partakers of it – you just have to be born into The Family to be an heir to The Covenant! God is so good that He has left a way and an open door so that *anyone* can be a member of His Family! The only condition is just like any other Blood Covenant between two families; you have to be a member of one of the families involved in The Covenant with each other. Father God also made a way that even though it has been 2,000 years since The Blood Covenant that He Cut with Mankind through His Firstborn, Jesus, it is still just as new and powerful and trustworthy today! *Remember, Blood Covenants are forever!*

Jesus from Nazareth, God's Chosen Covenant Representative always knew the seriousness of The Blood Covenant Ceremony, even when people around Him did not. Thousands of people followed Jesus *until He started speaking about "eat my flesh and drink my blood"* – **this was Blood Covenant Ceremony Talk!** *"Jesus said to them, "Very truly I tell you, unless you eat the flesh of the Son of Man and drink his blood, you have no life in you. 54 Whoever eats my flesh and drinks my blood has eternal life, and I will raise them up at the last day. . . From this time many of his disciples turned back and no longer followed him."* (John 6:53-54, 66 (NIV)

When He began to get *serious* about them and their relationship with Him and them coming into Blood Covenant with Him they left Him. And in Blood Covenant – *you never leave!*

When one comes into The Family and Covenant with God, just like all other Blood Covenants Cut, you receive a New Name! Just as in the Covenant Ceremonies of the past, the names were changed to reflect the family that you were coming into Covenant with, like the Smithjones or the Jonesmith. When you and I come into this New Blood Covenant that has been paid for, we are taking and receiving the new name of Christians! We have His Name and Him!

There is ALWAYS BLOOD in a Blood Covenant Ceremony. There were many in the Old Testament or Covenant; we have only touched on a few. Yet there was just one needed in the New

Testament or Covenant. And in order for a Covenant to take place, there ALWAYS has to be a Blood Covenant Ceremony to usher it into being. That is why Jesus did what He did, to fulfill The Blood Covenant Ceremony so that mankind would never have to again with God. Jesus said it best: *"It is finished!"*

Chapter Fifteen

COVENANTS OF TODAY

*Y*ou may have thought at one time or another within this book, *we don't have anything as serious and binding as The Blood Covenant Ceremony in our lives today!* **Oh, but Beloved of God, we really do!** The one that is the closest to what you have read throughout these pages is The Wedding of a man and a woman. *Actually, IT IS A BLOOD COVENANT CEREMONY!*

Let's begin again with the meaning of "Covenant." Total loyalty is essential by both parties in a Blood Covenant. The only way to get out of a Blood Covenant is through death. Covenant in the Hebrew is the word, *beriyth (ber-eeth')* OT:1285, **a compact made by passing between pieces of flesh: covenant, league. To cut, To divide.** You may be thinking right now, *Sister Jamie, I don't think from what I've read, that I've ever seen a Blood Covenant Ceremony in our day and age.* Well, let's look together.

When a man and a woman come to the place in their lives that they are going to marry, there is normally a wonderful thing that takes place, called a Wedding! The man and woman have many plans for this special Covenant Day.

The Covenant Site is chosen, where The Covenant Ceremony will be held. The Date and Time that The Covenant Ceremony will be decided upon in advance for all to come. Even invitations are created and sent to other family members so that they can come and witness and be a part of the merging of the two families that are coming into Covenant with each other. *Both sides of the Groom and Bride will attend and witness The Covenant between the two.*

The Conditions of The Covenant are discussed by the Bride and Groom. Conditions of The Covenant will be discussed and decided upon before the Ceremony. Examples of Condition would be if the Groom and Bride are going to stay in the town they both live in or if they will move, how many children they will have together, how they will handle their finances together, etc. And yet there will be **Covenant Conditions** that will need to be discussed and decided for *The actual Covenant Ceremony itself, which we refer to as a Wedding.* For example, what *"Vows"* will the Groom and Bride say and agree upon in The Ceremony? Will they repeat and speak out loud to each other and for the two sides of the families to hear, traditional vows or will they write their own to each other or both?

The Wedding Day

All gather together to witness this wonderful day when *two families will be coming together and becoming one.* **One family will be sitting on one side of the Church and the other family on the opposite side.**

The Groom and the Bride are representing each family at the Ceremony. These two *represent the best of these two families* coming in Covenant this day. When the Ceremony begins, the Groom will be at the front in the center of the aisle, awaiting his Bride. The music will begin and all will stand for the Bride to enter and walk down the center of the aisle. The Bride will meet her Groom in the center of the aisle.

Both Covenant Representatives (the Bride and Groom) stand in center of the two families. The Bride has walked between two sides of family, two sides of people, two sides of FLESH! The Bride has made the Covenant

Walk between two "pieces of flesh!" And the Bride meets her Groom in the Center of the "two fleshes" as they are coming into Covenant with each other. The Groom and Bride both stand in the center of the two families, between the "two pieces of flesh" where all the families can see and hear The Covenant being made.

The Promises and the Conditions of Covenant are Proclaimed while the Two Covenant Representatives are still standing in the center of the families. Again, the families are witnesses to this Covenant. The elders of The Blood Covenant Ceremonies were normally in the front due to their positions in the family. And likewise, in our Blood Covenants of Today (Weddings) the "elders", the fathers, mothers and grandparents of the two families are escorted in between the two families (the "two pieces of flesh") down the aisle. And then seated at the front and are honored by the families. Then one will hear the words of The Blood Covenant coming from both Covenant Representatives (the Groom and Bride.) *I pledge to never leave, nor forsake you. I promise to be with and you only, to have no other before you. You shall leave your father and mother and cleave to your wife. I will stay with you in the good and bad. I marry you today and will be with you forever, till death parts us.*

This Beloved, is Covenant Conditions and they are made by The Covenant Representatives (the Groom and Bride) in view of the two families in the center of them, in the center of the "two pieces of flesh" during a Wedding! Also, a ring is given to symbolize "all that I am I give to you today." Remember, what is vowed in Covenant in the Blood Covenant Ceremonies we have gone over throughout this Book:

All that I am and who I am, I give to you. I give you all my authority. You may use my authority to live your life. You have my authority now and I have yours.

I give you all my strength. Your enemies are now mine. I'll fight for you even if I die. When you go to battle I will always be by your side fighting alongside you and for you and your family, even to the death.

I will stand with you in the midst of death. This is forever. I will stand with you. I cannot and will not ever break my promise and Covenant with you.

I, as the chosen representative on behalf of my family, promise to uphold this Covenant with your family! I will and so will my family, so help me God!

And these Vows of The Covenant are the same meanings as to what has always been professed by Two Covenant Representatives (a Groom and a Bride) in a Wedding. Yes, Beloved you have been witnessing Blood Covenant Ceremonies all along! Covenant has always been important to God and they still are today. They are serious and they are forever, till death do you part! And that's the ONLY WAY to break a Blood Covenant, thousands of years ago and now!

The Names are Combined by the Two. Normally the Bride takes her Husband's name or combines hers with his last name.

The Covenant Meal I know in my and Dewayne's Wedding we partook of Communion. It is served to The Groom and Bride during The Blood Covenant Ceremony (Wedding). The bread and the juice are a symbol of Jesus Christ's Body and His Blood Covenant Ceremony for us and of His Covenant Cut He made to receive us as His Bride. Then what we call a Wedding Reception takes place after The Covenant Ceremony is complete. In The Blood Covenant Ceremony this feast is called **The Covenant Meal, shared with both families that have come into Covenant with each other and witnessed The Covenant Ceremony.**

As in Blood Covenant Ceremonies, the Covenant Representatives join their wrists together, uniting flesh to flesh. So are the Covenant Representatives (the Groom and the Bride) bodies joined flesh to flesh on their Wedding Night.

Now you may be thinking, what about The Blood? Well, during The Covenant Ceremonies in The Bible when a man and a woman married, if there was *any* thought by the Groom that his Bride was not a virgin after their Wedding Night, it could be brought before the Religious Leaders. **And what would be the evidence that the Groom would have that his Bride had been with another? <u>BLOOD</u>!**

"He has accused her of shameful conduct, saying, "I discovered that your daughter was not a virgin." But <u>here is the proof of my daughter's virginity.'</u> <u>Then they must spread her bed sheet before the elders.</u>" Deuteronomy 22:17 (NLT)

Blood would be shed The Covenant Night after The Blood Covenant Ceremony through the sexual relations of the Groom and Bride on their bed sheet. And if there was NOT BLOOD on those sheets after their sexual union, The Covenant would be broken, for the Bride was not a virgin and therefore all that was promised throughout The Conditions of Covenant was null and void. The Bride and her family deceived the Groom and his family.

There you have it. . . *A Wedding IS A Blood Covenant Ceremony!*

Chapter Sixteen

WHY DO IT

*J*esus is absolutely in Love with His Bride. Nothing could stand in His Way from getting to Her and having Her. He is waiting on Her and He is awaiting His Wedding Day. He has been waiting on His Bride for over 2,000 years! He would do <u>anything</u> for Her *and did everything instead!*

So when asked if He would go and Complete The New Blood Covenant Ceremony to get His Bride, I imagine that He would say,

Father, I'll go and I'll not only be The Blood Covenant Representative. . . I'll be The Covenant Animal. . . I'll even be The Covenant Blood. I'll give My Life For Hers and when I do, She'll get Her life back and have life more abundantly! She is My Destiny and I am Hers. I'll never leave Her or forsake Her. And when The Covenant is Complete, and It Is Finished, I'll go and Prepare a Place for Her to be with Me forever eternally!

Why did Jesus fight so hard and suffer so much? Because He Loves You and He *Is In Love With You!* He thinks you are wonderful. He thinks you are beautiful inside and out. He thinks you are smart and courageous. He thinks you are the best at anything and everything. He finds no fault in you. When He looks at you, He sees you through His Blood Covenant, and ALL was made RIGHT in that Blood Covenant

Ceremony! So He sees you as Right and in Right Standing with Him. He simply adores you, Bride! He simply, wholly and utterly Loves You!

Be Ready for Him! He's coming to get His Bride and She is to be ready and waiting for Him. Keep yourself clean by repenting. He wants us to be a Bride without a *spot or blemish.* And if you are a little dirty, The Blood of The Covenant that you have read about in this Book will wash you, if you let it.

Everything that Father God has done through Blood Covenants throughout history and all that Jesus did in The New Blood Covenant Ceremony was done for their Brides! Father God's is Israel and Jesus' is Us, The Church, His Bride. Everything has always been about their Brides! They have always been faithful to their Brides and they ALWAYS WILL. *Why?* Because They are in Blood Covenant with them! And when you are in Covenant, you don't quit, you don't leave, you don't give up, you always love, always hope, you are there. . . *always!*

I encourage you today to begin your love affair with your Bridegroom, Jesus. He is so deep and so wide and just too amazing for our English words. Surrender, or let me say it this way. . . *let go, just let yourself go and give your ALL to Him! Why? Because you can trust Him, because he gave it all up for you, even when you didn't know that He did! He's my Best Friend. He loves me no matter what. And in closing, I just want to write, I love you Jesus! You dazzle me—always have and always will. I adore You and appreciate all that You have done for me. I did it! I finally did it! I finally wrote Your Book! I pray that this book blesses Your Heart! It's been my privilege to do so!*

Until the Next Book, I love you deeply, Bride of Christ, The Beloved of God!

Keep Getting Ready, Church; Jesus is Coming! - Jamie

One Last Thing. . .

*A*dam and Eve had a wonderful Covenant with God. And then one day they both decided to commit high treason and pledged their allegiance to their enemy (the Devil.) When they chose the devil's word over God's command, they sinned. Man surrendered their rights to **an angel (the devil.)** Because Adam and Eve did this, it set in motion a Manner or Way for all Mankind.

When a man or woman dies without accepting The New Blood Covenant that Jesus paid for, they must follow the way that all the "Fallen Angels" that serve Satan go. Man has to go to the place that was prepared for the angels that rebelled against God go.

> *"Then he will say to those on his left, 'Depart from me, you who are cursed, **into the eternal fire prepared for the devil and his angels."** Matthew 25:41(NIV)*

Hell was prepared for the rebellious angels that followed Satan. And since Man followed an angel (the Devil) in the Garden of Eden, all of Adam and Eve's descendants are born into that rebellion and under that Covenant broken by Man. Therefore, if man dies without God, man goes where the angels that followed the Devil go. A man who follows the Devil goes to the place prepared for the Devil and his angels. Some men follow an angel all their lives and therefore have to go where the angel's (the Devil's) place is.

"For God did not spare even the angels who sinned. He threw them into hell, in gloomy pits of darkness, where they are being held until the day of judgment.
5 And God did not spare the ancient world—except for Noah and the seven others in his family. Noah warned the world of God's righteous judgment. So God protected Noah when he destroyed the world of ungodly people with a vast flood. 6 Later, God condemned the cities of Sodom and Gomorrah and turned them into heaps of ashes. He made them an example of what will happen to ungodly people." 2 Peter 2:4-6 (NLT)

But you don't have to follow an angel, and a fallen angel, at that! You can choose to follow God and His Son, Jesus! God sent Jesus to pay for and get back ALL THAT WE LOST IN THE GARDEN OF EDEN! That is why He did all that He did in The Blood Covenant Ceremony! He was making a Way for you and me to be with Him in Heaven and not with the Devil and his angels in Hell! You can receive *EVERYTHING that was purchased for you in the New Blood Covenant, paid for by our Big Brother, Jesus!*
The Lord wants you, and He has great plans for you and your life. Begin your New Covenant and life with Him. Romans 10:9-10 tells us:

"That if you confess with your mouth, 'Jesus is Lord,' and believe in your heart that God raised him from the dead, you will be saved. For it is with your heart that you believe and are justified, and it is with your mouth that you confess and are saved."

Put your trust in Him. Don't put Him off any longer. He wants you. You've been on His mind so much. And no matter what you have done, or even where you are right now as you read this, He wants you. Will you receive Him? I believe this is your moment to get things completely right with God! Believe these words with all your heart and confess them with your mouth out loud so that you can hear yourself. And mean it and say,

"Jesus, I know I have done wrong and that I am a sinner and I need a Savior. I believe You died on a cross for my sins and that You were buried for three days and then rose from the dead. I ask You to come into my life and save me, free me, and clean me. I confess today that You are Lord of my life. I will follow You for the rest of my days. In Jesus Name, I believe I receive. Amen."

If you said that prayer and you meant it, you have just come into the Bride of Christ! Your name has been written in the Lamb's Book of Life. You have made the most important decision of your whole life! Get yourself a Bible. Any translation is wonderful. We read them all. Some that are written in our modern day language are *The New International Version (NIV), The Amplified Bible (AMP), The New King James Version (NKJV), and The Living Bible (TLB).* If for any reason you cannot get yourself a Bible right now, please contact Jamie Carte Ministries. It would be our honor to get you a Bible and mail it to you, postage paid. Please use JCM's contact information to do so.

If you just for the first time gave your life to God or you have returned to Him and committed to give Him your all, we want you to know that we are so very happy for you! Make sure you get yourself into a Spirit-filled Church, one that praises and worships the Lord Jesus and teaches the Bible in its fullness, and one that is truly alive. Start asking Jesus where He wants you to attend and He'll show you. Also, start reading your Bible every day and praying (talking to Him) every day.

Once you have received Jesus Christ as your Lord and Savior, it is the Will of the Lord for you to have the fullness of the Holy Spirit. Acts 1:4-5 (NIV) reads:

*"On one occasion, while he was eating with them, he gave them this command: 'Do not leave Jerusalem, but wait for the gift my Father promised, which you have heard me speak about. **For John baptized with water, but in a few days you will be baptized with the Holy Spirit.'"***

Then in Acts 2:4 what Jesus said happened!

"All of them were filled with the Holy Spirit and began to speak in other tongues as the Spirit enabled them."

When you are baptized in the Holy Spirit, you will have evidence of it by speaking in tongues, just like they did on the day of Pentecost. When you pray in tongues, you pray in the Spirit. You are letting the Holy Spirit pray through your spirit. If you desire the infilling of the Holy Spirit, pray the prayer below and believe you will receive:

"Lord Jesus, I am a new creature in Christ and I ask you to baptize me in the Holy Spirit and enable me to be a powerful witness to the World about you. I believe that I receive this gift just like the disciples did on the day of Pentecost."

If you have made these important decisions today, please let us know at Jamie Carte Ministries. We want to celebrate with you and we'd like to send you some Free Resources to bless you and help you in your New Journey with The Lord! Please contact us at:

Jamie Carte Ministries, JCM

P. O. Box 120

Hico, WV 25854

www.jamiecarte.org

The Lord Jesus Loves You So Very Much! And He Will Never Leave You! Remember, He's In Blood Covenant With You Now! God Bless You, Greatly Beloved!

Jamie Carte Ministries, (JCM)
Who We Are

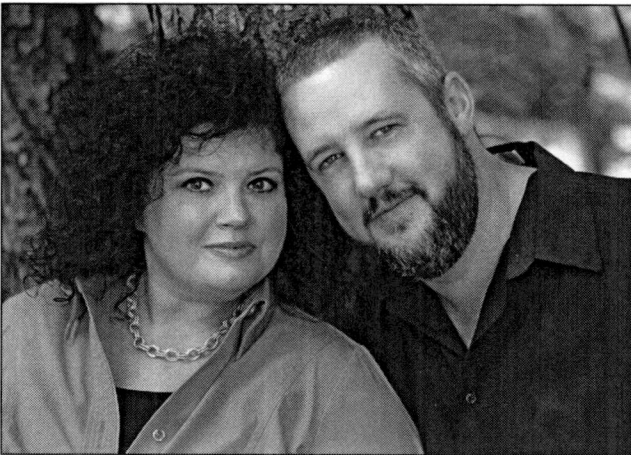

*D*ewayne and Jamie Carte are both Ordained Ministers and the Senior Ministers of Jamie Carte Ministries. They were brought together by God when they met at their church. Dewayne and Jamie married in December 1999. Jamie has served in the position of a Youth Minister for eight years and Dewayne and Jamie both have served as Youth Ministers together for four years. Jamie has served in the position of Praise and Worship Leader for eight years and has served in the position of Ministerial Staff for six years, while Dewayne has served in the positions of Ministerial Staff and an Elder for nine years.

In 2003 The Lord began to show Dewayne and Jamie that the call on their lives was broadening to go into all the World and evangelize the lost and assist the Bride of Christ, The Church to enter into a healthy, loving, and strong relationship with Jesus Christ. They stepped out by faith in following the call on their lives and formed Jamie Carte Ministries (JCM), a Non-Profit Organization. Dewayne serves as the President and Overseer of JCM while Jamie serves as the Vice President. Dewayne and Jamie live at Hico, WV.

This Ministry is called to go into the Bride's chamber and bandage Her wounds and pains with the ointment of the Bridegroom. To assist the Bride of Christ as She steps into Her wedding gown. We are called to send messages from the Bridegroom to the Bride as She awaits Her Love in Her chambers. JCM is called through God's Word to reveal and deliver the glorious mysteries of Him by the Holy Spirit to the Bride of Christ. To bring forth freedom through the revelations of God's Word that have been hidden for ages and generations (Colossians 1:25-28).

We are in a mission to assist the Bride of Christ in reaching Her reliance in what Her Bridegroom says (the Word Of God). To aid Her in not just reading the Word of God, but becoming all that it says She is. We are committed to bringing the Bride of Christ into a healed, healthy and trusting relationship with Her Bridegroom, Jesus Christ. On the Wedding Day, She will stand boldly before Her Bridegroom with integrity, boldness, and complete freedom. The messages provided by the Holy Spirit through Jamie Carte Ministries will assist Her in the preparation of the Wedding Day, which is the Rapture of The Church.

Dewayne and Jamie both minister The Word of God through Speaking Engagements, JCM's Weekly TV Ministry, *"GETTING READY!,"* through Daily Internet teachings, and teachings of The Word of God through a FREE Monthly

Teaching Mailout from JCM. Also, other avenues JCM ministers is through FREE teachings on DVD and Audio CD's that are available to the Public and are distributed all over the World, and JCM is avid about reaching out to help clothe, feed and do Public Outreaches to those in need and are active in doing so. If we can serve you in any way, it would be our honor to do so.

You can contact us at:

Jamie Carte Ministries (J.C.M.)

P.O. Box 120

Hico, WV 25854

www.jamiecarte.org

1-304-658-4720

You May Also Connect With Us By E-mail at:

www.contact@jamiecarte.org

www.prayer@jamiecarte.org

Or Connect With Jamie Carte

Ministries on FaceBook, Twitter

and MySpace

We'd Love To Hear From You!

THE END NOTES

i.   Galatians 5:13 (KJV)
li.   [1]Acts 10:34 (KJV)
iii.   [1]Matthew 22:36-39
iv.   [1]Proverbs 18:22
v.   [1]Philippians 4:19
vi.   [1]1 Peter 5:7
vii.   [1]Genesis 22:14, 1 John 5:14,15
viii. [1]Matthew 9:36 (Amplified Bible) ". . . He was moved with pity and sympathy for them, because they were bewildered (harassed and distressed and dejected and helpless), like sheep without a shepherd."

ix.   [1]Matthew 26:53 (Contemporary English Version) "Don't you know that I could ask my Father, and right away he would send me more than twelve armies of angels?"
x.   [1]John 10:10, Ephesians 3:20
xi.   [1]1 Samuel 12:12 (NLT) ". . . you came to me and said that you wanted a king to reign over you, even though the LORD your God was already your king."

CPSIA information can be obtained at www.ICGtesting.com
Printed in the USA
BVOW022032160613

323401BV00006B/9/P

9 781626 974036